THE HERITAGE TRUST ESTATE ADMINISTRATION BOOT CAMP

A COMPLETE GUIDE ON HOW TO PROBATE AND ADMINISTER AN ESTATE IN BRITISH COLUMBIA

NICOLE GARTON, LLB, TEP

The Heritage Trust Estate Administration Boot Camp
Copyright © 2019 by Nicole Garton, LLB, TEP

All rights reserved. No part of this publication may be reproduced, distributed, or transmitted in any form or by any means, including photocopying, recording, or other electronic or mechanical methods, without the prior written permission of the author, except in the case of brief quotations embodied in critical reviews and certain other non-commercial uses permitted by copyright law.

Tellwell Talent
www.tellwell.ca

ISBN
978-0-2288-1971-4 (Paperback)

Table of Contents

Introduction vii

Chapter 1   From the Act to Action 1
    Introduction 1

Chapter 2   "Executor", "Administrator", "Administrator With Will Annexed",
             or "Personal Representative", and Types of Grants 4
    Introduction 4
    Executor (sometimes referred to as "Executrix" if female) 4
    Administrator (Without Will Annexed) 5
    Administrator (With Will Annexed) 6
    Personal Representative 7
    Other Types of Grants 7
    Common Form or Solemn Form 7

Chapter 3   Fiduciary Duties: Do You Want to Assume this Role? 9
    Personal Representatives: Powers, Duties, and Liabilities 9
    Intermeddling 12
    Possible Renunciation 13
    Executor and Administrator Fees 13
    Citations 14
    Subpoena For Testamentary Document 15

Chapter 4   Is the Will a Valid Will? 24
    Introduction 24
    Testamentary Capacity 25
    Undue Influence 27
    Curative Provisions 29
    Codicil & Outside Documents 30

Chapter 5 Initial Responsibilities of the Personal Representative 31
  Introduction 31
  Arranging the Funeral and Dealing with the Remains 32
  Insolvent Estates 33
  Locating the Will 34
  Reviewing the Will 36
  Safeguarding Assets 37
  Gathering Information 39
  Listing Assets and Liabilities...39
  Identifying the Beneficiaries and Intestate Successors of the Estate........ 42
  Ongoing Obligation to Maintain Accounts and Expenses......................... 42
  Income Taxes...43

Chapter 6 Is an Estate Grant Necessary? 54

Chapter 7 It's All in the Family...56
  Introduction 56
  Definition of a Spouse 56
  Children...57

Chapter 8 Where There's a Will... There's a Way..58
  Introduction 58
  Form P1 Notice of Proposed Application in Relation to Estate 58
  Form P2 Submission for Estate Grant..63
  Form P3 or P4 – Affidavit of Applicant 65
  Form P9 Affidavit of Delivery.. 66
  Form P10 Affidavit of Assets and Liabilities 66
  Application for Grant of Administration with Will Annexed......................71

Chapter 9 Where There's No Will... There's Still a Way 102
  Introduction 102
  Missing Intestate Successors 103
  Bonds...103
  Estate Grant Application...103
  Form P1 Notice of Proposed Application in Relation to Estate 104
  Form P2 Submission for Estate Grant..109
  Form P5 Affidavit of Applicant for Grant of Administration Without Will Annexed ...110
  Form P9 Affidavit of Delivery.. 111
  Form P10 Affidavit of Assets and Liabilities 111

Chapter 10 Obtaining the Estate Grant 135
   Swearing Affidavits 135
   Checklist 135
   Probate Fees 135

Chapter 11 Post-Grant Procedures: Transfer of Assets and Distribution of the Estate ... 137
   Introduction 137
   Distribution Limitation Period 137
   Liquidating Assets 138
   Creditors 139
   Income Tax Returns 140
   Approval and Releases 141
   Passing of Accounts 142

Chapter 12 Your Role as the Trustee 155

Chapter 13 Estates of Indigenous People 157

Chapter 14 Closing Matters 159
   Further Resources 159

Terms and Definitions 161

Introduction

You have been named the executor or administrator of an estate. We first would like to express our condolences for your loss. Losing a friend or family member can be very hard. Being appointed the executor or administrator of an estate can seem like an added burden when dealing with your grief and loss. We wrote this guide especially for you. We know that being an executor or administrator can be challenging, overwhelming, and time-consuming. Before accepting this position, we strongly urge you to read this guide and understand your role and obligations.

Being the executor or administrator of your loved one's estate can be a great way to honour their memory, but it does come with many legal expectations. There are many deadlines, forms, and processes that must be followed. We strongly urge you to consider if you are able to manage the estate and all the tasks that come with it.

By reading this guide, you will gain a better sense of what it means to be a personal representative of an estate and all the associated rights, duties, and tasks. This guide will walk you through all the steps of being an executor or administrator, from being appointed to distributing the estate. Should you choose to accept this role, this book will guide you through the administration process and can save you hundreds of dollars in legal and administrative fees. By following this guide, you will administer the estate in compliance with BC laws and regulations.

This guide does not substitute legal advice. If there are complex matters that arise with the estate during any point of the administration, or if you have legal questions that are relevant to the estate, we recommend that you seek legal advice.

We kindly remind you that this book only covers the specific legal matters of estate administration. For all accounting or financial matters, we recommend seeking the advice of an accountant or other professional.

Chapter 1

From the Act to Action

Introduction

British Columbia has had some relatively recent changes to its governing legislation in the area of wills and estates. Prior to March 31, 2014, the province was governed by the *Estate Administration Act* (RSBC 1996, c 122), the *Wills Variation Act* (RSBC 1996, c 490), the *Wills Act* (RSBC 1996, c 489), and the *Probate Recognition Act,* (RSBC 1991, c 376). These pieces of legislation were all replaced by one complete Act: the *Wills, Estates, and Succession Act* (SBC 2009, c 13, "WESA"). The province also enacted new probate rules that were inserted into sections 25-1 to 25-16 of the British Columbia *Supreme Court Civil Rules.*

WESA, the conglomerate Act, was the province's attempt to streamline the process of estate administration. The new legislation updated antiquated rules and modernized the way that estates may be handled. For example, there is now a way to interpret computerized documents as testamentary in nature and apply to have them submitted for probate purposes.

Some notable changes include:

- A person is now able to make a valid will at the age of 16 rather than 19 years old.

- The distribution scheme changed to a parentelic chart (explained in Chapter 9 of this guide) to ensure that there is a cut-off rather than continuing to search for a next of kin indefinitely. If there is no heir that can be found when you reach the fourth degree in the parentelic chart, then the estate reverts to the Crown (provincial government).

- The Court has the jurisdiction to declare that a document is a valid will even when it has not met the formal requirements of a will in British Columbia. Therefore, memos or notes, recorded messages, computer documents, or even emails may be submitted to the Court to decide whether the deceased person intended these documents to represent their testamentary intentions and to effectively "cure" the document to have it recognized as a valid will.

- The definition of what constitutes a "spouse" by law has expanded to include married spouses and people who have lived together in a marriage-like relationship for at least 2 years.

- Furthermore, there is more clarity on how spouses cease to be defined as spouses. In the case of a marriage, parties cease to be spouses if an event occurs that causes an interest in family property, as defined in Part 5 [Property Division] of the *Family Law Act*, to arise. If the spouses are common-law, the spousal relationship is terminated as soon as one or both of them end the relationship.

- If there is a gift in a will to a person who is no longer defined as a spouse, or if a will-maker has made an appointment in their will to have their spouse appointed as the executor and they cease being spouses, that appointment or gift is revoked and treated as through the ex-spouse had predeceased the will-maker, unless there is a specific contrary intention expressed in the will.

- Importantly, WESA has changed the previous rule that getting married will revoke a will. Anyone who is married after March 31, 2014 and has an existing will can retain that will without consequence (other than being subject to WESA). Prior to WESA, if you had a pre-existing will and you got married, that will would automatically be revoked. If you hadn't made a new will after you were married, then you would die intestate (meaning there is no will to probate). It is important to note that if you had a will in place and were married before March 31, 2014, that will is considered revoked.

- The devolution of the estate on an intestacy (without a will) has changed drastically with WESA. If the deceased died after March 31, 2014, the spouse of the deceased will inherit the first $300,000 of the estate and has the option of buying out the family home within the first 180 days after the date of receiving the estate grant. However, if there are children of the deceased who are not also children of the surviving spouse, the $300,000 inheritance to the surviving spouse is reduced to $150,000.

- Under the old law, there was a specific scheme that could be used to determine survivorship: when two people died at the same time and it was impossible to tell who died first (to determine whose estate to probate and who survived the other), the youngest person was deemed to have survived the older person. WESA has introduced a new rubric where each person is deemed to survive the other.

- If a beneficiary in the will does not survive the deceased by at least five days, they are now deemed to have predeceased the deceased and do not receive under the will.

Please note that if an existing will was prepared prior to March 31, 2014, that will is not invalidated by the introduction of WESA. The existing will is, however, interpreted and probated under the new probate rules and according to WESA, so it is important to clarify if there are any conflicts with the laws and changes that came into force.

Chapter 2

"Executor", "Administrator", "Administrator With Will Annexed", or "Personal Representative", and Types of Grants

Introduction

The administration of estates can be confusing. Understanding terminology is key to succeeding in navigating the nuances embedded in the rules, forms, law, and legislation.

Executor (sometimes referred to as "Executrix" if female)

An executor is a person or an institution who is appointed by a will-maker to administer an estate in accordance with the terms set out in the will. There can be co-executors (two or more) if more than one person was appointed in the will, but keep in mind that co-executors must agree on all decisions (unless there is a provision in the will stating otherwise or there is a "majority rules" clause). Due to the default rule that co-executors must agree, it is important that either they get along or one of them renounces their right to apply as executor of the estate. Renouncing executor rights might also happen if one of the executors lives far away from the where the deceased was domiciled. The physical separation might make it difficult or inconvenient for the co-executors to make decisions and sign documents that need to be attended to throughout the estate administration. If the co-executors cannot agree on something, they will need to apply to the court to receive directions on how to proceed.

The executor has specific responsibilities and duties that they must perform if they accept the appointment. This guide will expand upon these and other obligations in the following chapter. It is important to note that if there is no will, there is no executor; therefore, there is an inextricable link between being an executor and the existence of a valid will.

In the drafting of many wills, the executor is referred to as the "trustee".

A will typically appoints an alternate executor if their first choice of executor is unable or unwilling to act.

Notably, because the will appoints the executor, the executor is the only title that speaks from the date of death. That is, the deceased person or will-maker chose the specific executor or co-executors and therefore, as soon as that person has died, the executor can immediately act as the personal representative of the estate.

Administrator (Without Will Annexed)

An administrator is a person (or more than one person) who will carry out the administration of the estate where there is no will and the deceased has therefore died intestate. Because an administrator has not been appointed by any testamentary instrument, someone must step up to apply to become the administrator of the estate. WESA sets out a list of priority among applicants at section 130 as follows:

130   If a person dies without a will, the court may grant administration of the deceased person's estate to one or more of the following persons in the following order of priority:

    a) The spouse of the deceased person or a person nominated by the spouse;

    b) A child of the deceased person having the consent of a majority of the children of the deceased person;

    c) A person nominated by a child of the deceased person if that person has the consent of a majority of the deceased person's children;

    d) A child of the deceased person not having the consent of a majority of the deceased person's children;

    e) An intestate successor other than the spouse or child of the deceased person, having the consent of the intestate successors representing a majority in interest of the estate, including the intestate successor who applies for a grant of administration;

    f) An intestate successor other than the spouse or child of the deceased person, not having the consent of the intestate successors representing a majority in interest of the estate, including the intestate successor who applies for a grant of administration;

    g) Any other person the court considers appropriate to appoint, including, without limitation, and subject to the Public Guardian and Trustee's consent, the Public Guardian and Trustee.

Since there was no executor appointed in this scenario, the person who is applying to be the administrator of the estate does not have the authority to represent the estate upon the death of the deceased. The appointment of adminstrator does not come fully into force until an estate grant has been declared by the Supreme Court registry. The administrator cannot hold themselves out as the personal representative of the estate until the estate grant is obtained. If no one applies, the court may appoint an official administrator. Note that until the personal representative, which encompasses both the executor and administrator, is appointed the estate is legally vested in the court.

Administrator (With Will Annexed)

Sometimes there is a will of the deceased that does not make a provision for an appointment of an executor. Other times, there is a will that has appointed an executor but that executor, for any reason, may decide that they do not want to be appointed or cannot be appointed. They may have predeceased the will-maker, they may be ill or mentally incompetent, or they may just not have the time or energy to take on such a large and important task. In this instance, the will still needs to be submitted for probate, but someone needs to carry it through and administer the estate.

For an administration with will annexed, the applicant will need to get Consents from all of the beneficiaries named in the will to proceed with the application. There is no prescribed form of Consent and the Consents do not need to be filed with the estate grant application; however, the originals should be retained and kept in safekeeping in case they are needed later on in the process to prove that the administrator has the Consents.

WESA also sets out a list of priority of applicants to apply, at section 131:

131   If a person dies leaving a will, and the executor named in the will renounces executorship or is unable or unwilling to apply for a grant of probate, or if no executor is named in the will, the court may grant administration with will annexed to one or more of the following persons in the following order for priority:

a) A beneficiary who applies having the consent of the beneficiaries representing a majority in interest of the estate, including the applicant;

b) A beneficiary who applies not having the consent of the beneficiaries representing a majority in interest of the estate;

c) Any other person the court considers appropriate to appoint, including, without limitation, and subject to the Public Guardian and Trustee's consent, the Public Guardian and Trustee.

An administrator with or without will annexed will acquire the same duties and responsibilities as an appointed executor would once they have obtained the estate grant.

The only difference is that the court may require that a security bond be posted in court by an administrator since that person was not chosen by the deceased to be their personal representative. Security is only required when there are interests in the estate that are held by a minor or by a mentally incompetent person, or if the court requires it.

Personal Representative

Generally, any of the above-noted titles can be referred to as a "Personal Representative". This term encompasses all of the types of administrators of estates and can be used interchangeably with executor/executrix, administrator, and administrator with will annexed.

Other Types of Grants

There are other types of estate grants that can be sought, though they are beyond the scope of this book. Several that you should be aware of are the following:

1. Resealing a Foreign Grant

   a. This is the process of having the local provincial court confirm a Grant of Probate from another jurisdiction. This includes any member of the British Commonwealth of Nations, any states of the USA, or Hong Kong.

2. Ancillary Grant of Probate or Ancillary Grant of Administration (With or Without Will Annexed)

   a. This type of grant may be required when you cannot reseal a foreign grant. An ancillary grant can be granted to the personal representative appointed by the foreign court.

3. Administration in Special Circumstances

   a. This type of estate administration grant may be required where the person entitled is out of country or the persons entitled are not yet determined.

4. Administration Pending Legal Proceedings

   a. This type of estate administration grant may be required where the person appointed is pending a proceeding, for example, the validity of the will.

5. Administration of Unadministered Estate

   a. This type of estate administration grant will be required where the administrator dies during the administration of the estate.

Common Form or Solemn Form

When you are dealing with a will and not an intestacy, the usual application procedure for an estate grant is "Proof in Common Form". This application is submitted to the court registry by way of a "Desk Order", which means that you do not have to go to court and appear in front of a judge to get the grant approved. If there are circumstances that require you to submit the will under a procedure called "Proof in Solemn Form", then a court application will be necessary. Solemn form provides more protection for a will so that the estate grant cannot later be set aside. If there is any doubt to the validity of the will or if there is opposition to it by someone having filed a Notice of Dispute, then the executor must proceed to prove the will in solemn form. The validity of a will can be challenged on the basis of undue influence or lack of testamentary capacity, witnessing requirements not being adhered to, breach of statute, or reason to believe there is a later will. Proof in solemn form requires proof of the will in a hearing or trial, after which the court pronounces for the force and validity of the will in solemn form (Supreme Court Civil Rule 25-1(5)).

Chapter 3

Fiduciary Duties: Do You Want
to Assume this Role?

Personal Representatives: Powers, Duties, and Liabilities

The role of a personal representative of an estate is outlined at sections 142 and 149 of WESA:

142 (1) A personal representative has the same authority over the estate in respect of which the personal representative is appointed as the deceased person would have if living, subject to

a) A contrary intention appearing in the will of the deceased person, and

b) This or any other enactment.

(2) A personal representative must exercise authority to

a) Administer and distribute the estate in respect of which the personal representative is appointed,

b) Account to beneficiaries, creditors and others to whom the personal representative has at law a duty to account, and

c) Perform any other duties imposed on the personal representative by the will of the deceased person or by law.

149 (1) A personal representative is liable, to the extent of the assets belonging to the estate that come into the personal representative's possession or control, for the wrongful acts and omissions or breaches of legal duty of the deceased person, subject to this or any other enactment to the contrary.

(2) Subjection (1) does not make liable an executor who renounces probate or administration or whose rights are reserved by a representation grant and who has not intermeddled in the estate.

Serious consideration should be made before assuming the role of personal representative. There are a number of challenges that should be deliberated, including the amount of time it will take, not only in terms of the daily or weekly time spent being representative but the time it will take to finally wind up the estate. Depending on the complexity of the estate, this could take years, especially if there are ongoing trusts created within the will. You should also consider the relationships between the beneficiaries and intestate successors and if there are any foreseeable conflicts in dynamics between these people which would make it more difficult for them to agree or approve your dealings. Another factor to think about is the type and extent of assets and liabilities that will need to be dealt with. Finally, it is extremely important to think about the potential personal liability that could arise if there are any mistakes made during the course of the administration. There is a potential for a breach of trust under statute and, if you take the wrong turn, you may have to personally pay any damages that arise, which could be significant depending on the estate.

An executor has responsibilities imposed upon them by common law and statute. By law, the executor must act with the level of skill and prudence that would be expected by a reasonable person of business. A professional executor will furthermore be held to the standard of the profession. Therefore, there is a high threshold for getting the job done right.

If you are appointed as an executor by a will, your authority to act comes directly from the will, as well as WESA (expanded upon above). There may be duties specifically described in the will that the executor must follow. Additionally, the following are generally included as duties of the executor:

- Making appropriate funeral arrangements;

- Gathering up, taking possession of, or controlling the deceased's assets and safeguarding those assets in trust for the estate;

- Paying the debts and liabilities of the estate or making other provisions for those debts and liabilities;

- Providing the proper notice to the beneficiaries under the will and the intestate successors of the estate;

- Managing and administering the estate by acting personally, subject to any powers of delegation which in some circumstances may be permitted;

- If so authorized under the will and the *Trustee Act,* RSBC 1996, c 464, ensuring the investment of estate assets;

The Heritage Trust Estate Administration Boot Camp

- Maintaining an even hand and acting impartially to beneficiaries and intestate successors;

- Taking care of the assets of the estate in accordance with the will or other memorandum;

- Bringing, maintaining, or continuing litigation actions on behalf of the estate, where necessary;

- Maintaining a proper and detailed accounting of the estate and always being prepared to account to the beneficiaries and creditors of the estate; and

- Final distribution of the assets of the estate to the beneficiaries in accordance with the will.

You may often hear the word "fiduciary" in relation to the executor of the estate. A fiduciary is a person (or a business) who has the power and obligation to act for the benefit of another under circumstances which require total trust, good faith, and honesty. A fiduciary relationship is of the highest degree of trust and must be strictly adhered to. Any breach of a fiduciary duty would allow a beneficiary to bring a court action against the executor, who would then potentially be personally liable to the extent of the breach.

Some of the fiduciary duties of a personal representative include:

- Carrying out the directions of the will,

- Always acting with the honesty and prudence of an average professional,

- Preserving the property of the will-maker,

- Providing an accurate and complete accounting,

- Not profiting from your position, and;

- Not delegating the decision making for the estate to someone else.

As an executor, you will have what is called an "executor's year" (which is a year from the date of the deceased's death) before you must distribute the deceased's estate to the beneficiaries. The reason for this executor's year is to give the executor an opportunity to identify and gather all the estate assets and to pay all debts.

For three years after the deceased's death, the estate can be treated as a separate taxpayer with respect to the income it earns. This tax treatment is only available to the extent that the estate, and the income earned by it, is not distributed to the beneficiaries during that period. It may be, depending on the income situation of each of the beneficiaries, that there is some advantage to having the estate not distribute assets to beneficiaries until after the third anniversary of the deceased's death. If some of the beneficiaries are already paying income tax at high marginal rates, there may be a significant tax saving if the estate files as a separate taxpayer and pays at the lowest possible marginal rates.

There is a strong potential for personal liability when one assumes the role of a personal representative. Common failures on the part of representative can happen easily, and may include the following:

- Arranging for funeral expenses that are unreasonable;

- Not doing a diligent search for all of the estate assets;

- Failing to protect, insure, and manage the estate assets;

- Not finding all of the estate liabilities, and/or not paying all those that are payable;

- Not arranging for the proper accounting of taxes and filing the appropriate tax returns;

- If nominated with the power to invest, not diligently investing estate assets for the benefit of the estate;

- Not clearly identifying all of the beneficiaries and/or intestate successors;

- Not adequately providing the beneficiaries with a proper accounting and eventual distribution of the estate.

If any of the above happen during the course of administering the estate, you will be personally responsible for the associated loss, the estate cannot cover the shortfall for you.

Intermeddling

If you are not yet sure if you intend to act as the personal representative, you must be extremely careful that you do not intermeddle in the estate before you make your decision. You cannot deal with any of the assets or liabilities of the estate or otherwise interfere or hold yourself out as the executor or administrator. If you do these things, you may be forced or compelled to continue to act as the personal representative and see things through until the end.

Intermeddling is defined as someone who has acted in relation to the deceased's property in a manner that would suggest that they have the intention of pursuing the role of personal representative. Note that arranging for a funeral is not defined as intermeddling; however, if you deal with any of the assets or liabilities or advise anyone that you are acting, you may not be able to renounce the executorship later on and may in turn become personally liable for any loss or damage to the estate.

Possible Renunciation

Even though you have been appointed under a will, you are not under any obligation to act as the executor of the estate if you do not want to (unless you have intermeddled in the estate). You should be fully aware that assuming the appointment of personal representative is not an easy task. It may take a long time to wind up the estate. There may be difficulties between beneficiaries or in obtaining information from financial institutions and if you are not familiar with the relevant laws and rules, it can be a challenge to learn how to navigate the court system. A potential executor may renounce and abandon their right to obtain a grant of probate. This may be due to their age or a conflict of interest, or they may not want the burden of acting. Renunciation is governed by section 104 of WESA.

WESA provides that the renunciation of an executor must be unconditional. You fill out the prescribed Form P17 to be filed in the Supreme Court to prove to the court that you have decided not to act as executor, which will ultimately terminate the executorship. The Renunciation should be witnessed by a person who has no interest in the estate.

A renunciation is not actually complete until it is filed within the Probate Registry. It is therefore important to keep the original in a safe place until the estate grant application is submitted to the registry.

A sample Notice of Renunciation in Form P17 is included at the end of this chapter.

Executor and Administrator Fees

If you decide to accept the appointment of executor or apply to become the administrator of an estate, you are entitled to be compensated for performing that role.

The *Trustee Act* (RSBC 1996, c 464) outlines the schematic under which you can be paid for your time and efforts. There is a maximum fee of 5% of the gross aggregate value of the estate (which does not include any deductions for liabilities that the estate is responsible for), 5% of the income earned on the estate assets during your administration, and an annual 0.4% "care and management" fee based on the average market value of the estate you are administering. The "care and management" fee is traditionally sought only when there is an ongoing trust for the executor to administer according to the terms of the will.

It is prudent to note that the initial amount of 5% of the aggregate realized value is reserved for those estates that are very complicated and take a long time to distribute and administer. The executor or administrator must prove to the beneficiaries that the whole 5% is warranted, and the beneficiaries must approve the accounting of the personal representative before they are able to get paid. A more typical estate matter may warrant a fee of around 2% of the gross value of the estate. If there is more than one personal representative then the fees will need to be divided and split between them, by agreement or by court direction if an agreement cannot be reached.

The personal representative is additionally entitled to be reimbursed for any out-of-pocket expenses that were made during the administration of the estate. Best practice is to keep a journal with a running tally and receipts to back up expenses so that these disbursements can be claimed without disagreement from the beneficiaries.

While reasonable professional fees are proper estate expenses for which you may be reimbursed from the estate, fees for work that falls within the executor's duties which other professionals do on your behalf must be paid by you personally or be deducted from your fee.

Sometimes there is a clause in a will that grants the executor a specific fee or cash bequest for assuming the role of executor. In this case, the executor is entitled to that fee or bequest and not an additional amount or percentage under the *Trustee Act,* unless a contrary intention is included in the will or the beneficiaries all agree to the executor receiving further compensation. The executor will, however, still be compensated for any out-of-pocket expenses.

Note that any fees for compensation of being the personal representative are treated as employment income by the Canada Revenue Agency and are subject to income tax.

If the executor is also the sole residual beneficiary of the estate, it is likely not warranted to claim fees as executor since such fees would be treated as income for tax purposes.

Citations

You may be wondering what happens if an executor does not go ahead and apply for a grant of probate of a will. There is a way to force a person to either act as the executor or renounce if they have not taken any steps towards moving forward with the estate. Any person interested in the estate may serve a document called a Citation in Form P32, under the Supreme Court Civil Rules. This document requires the named executor in the will to either accept or renounce the probating of the will. Alternatively, if the individual who served the Citation does not want the named executor to accept or renounce, then the person issuing the Citation has to explain why the administration of the estate should not be granted to the executor. The person served with the Citation must respond within 14 days or obtain a grant of probate within six months of being served with the Citation. If they do not, they will be deemed to renounce their right to apply for probate and other people are then allowed to apply in place of the named executor. In this situation, Form P34 is used as an Affidavit of Deemed Renunciation.

Samples of Forms P32 and P34 can be found at the end of this chapter.

Subpoena For Testamentary Document

If you require access to a testamentary document that someone is in possession of and after asking them they refuse to provide the document, you may apply to the court by way of requisition using Form 35 for a subpoena. This requisition must be supported by an affidavit using Form 37. You can request a testamentary document, an authorization to obtain the estate or to reseal information, an estate, a foreign or resealed foreign grant, or a certified or notarized copy of a testamentary document.

Samples of Forms 35 and 37 can be found at the end of this chapter.

Nicole Garton, LLB, TEP

Form P17 (Rule 25-3(2))

No.
Court Registry: _____

In the Supreme Court of British Columbia

In the Matter of the Estate of *[legal name of deceased]*, deceased

NOTICE OF RENUNCIATION

WHEREAS the deceased, formerly of *[city, province]*, died on *[month, day, year]*, having made and duly executed a last will dated *[month, day, year]*, (the "will") and appointed *[name]* executor *[add, if applicable: and trustee]* of it:

I, *[name]*, hereby renounce executorship in relation to the will and declare that I have not intermeddled in the estate of the deceased and will not intermeddle in it with the intent to defraud creditors.

Date: *[month, day, year]*   _____
                                               Signature of renouncing executor
                                               [type or print name]

This notice of renunciation was signed by the renouncing executor in the presence of

WITNESS

[The witness to this acknowledgement must be at least 19 years of age.]

Name: _____ *[type or print name]*

Address: _____   _____
                                          Signature of Witness

Occupation: _____

Form P32 (Rule 25-11(1))

[style of proceeding]

In the Matter of the Estate of *[legal name of deceased]*, deceased

CITATION

[Rule 22-3 of the Supreme Court Civil Rules applies to all forms.]

To: *[name and address]*

This citation is issued by *[name of citor]* (the "citor") regarding the estate of *[legal name of deceased]*, (the "deceased"), who died on *[month, day, year]*.

This citation is issued in relation to the following document that is/is alleged to be a will of the deceased: *[describe document and its location, if known]*.

I believe the document exists because: *[set out basis for citor's belief]*.

You are required to obtain a grant of probate in relation to the above-noted will and comply with Rule 25-11(4) in the manner set out below.

The citor's address for service is: *[specify]*

[You must set out the street address of the address for service. One or both of a fax number and an email address may be given as additional addresses for service.]

Street address for service: *[specify]*

Fax number address for service (if any): *[specify]*

Email address for service (if any): *[specify]*

Telephone number: *[specify]*

Date: *[month, day, year]*.

_____

Signature of
[ ]   citor
[ ]   lawyer for citor

[type or print name]

[Note that a reference to "will" in this citation includes all documents that are included within the definition of "will" in the Wills, Estates and Succession Act.]

TAKE NOTICE THAT you must comply with Rule 25-11(4) of the Supreme Court Civil Rules.

To comply with Rule 25-11(4), you must do the following within 14 days after being served with this citation:

    (a)   if you have been issued a grant of probate, serve on the citor, by ordinary service, a copy of the grant;

    (b)   if paragraph (a) does not apply but you have filed a submission for estate grant, serve a copy of the filed application materials on the citor;

    (c)   if paragraphs (a) and (b) do not apply but you have delivered a notice under Rule 25-2(1), serve a copy of the notice documents on the citor;

    (d)   if none of paragraphs (a), (b) and (c) apply, serve on the citor an answer in Form P33.

AND TAKE NOTICE THAT, if you do not comply with Rule 25-11(4), one or more of the following may occur:

    (a)   you may be deemed to have renounced executorship under Rule 25-11(5);

    (b)   the citor or another person may apply for an estate grant in relation to the estate;

    (c)   an order under Rule 25-11(6) may be obtained.

The Heritage Trust Estate Administration Boot Camp

Form P34 (Rule 25-11(7))

This is the *[1st/2nd/3rd/etc.]* affidavit
of *[name]* in this case and was made
on *[month, day, year]*

[style of proceeding]

AFFIDAVIT OF DEEMED RENUNCIATION

[Rule 22-3 of the Supreme Court Civil Rules applies to all forms.]

I, *[name]*, of *[address]*, *[occupation]*, SWEAR (OR AFFIRM) THAT:

1 Attached to this affidavit and marked as Exhibit A is a copy of the citation I prepared (the "citation") in relation to the estate of *[legal name of deceased]*.

2 On *[month, day, year]*, at *[time of day]*, I served *[name of person served]* with the citation by handing it to and leaving it with that person at *[city and country]*.

[or]

2 In support of this affidavit is filed the affidavit of service dated *[month, day, year]* of *[name of person swearing affidavit of service]* in which that person swears that the citation was served on *[name of person served]*.

3 I have not received service of any of the documents referred to in Rule 25-11(4) and at least 14 days have elapsed since the citation was served on *[name of person served]*.

[or]

3 *[name of person served]* served on me, under Rule 25-11(4)(b)(iii)(B), the answer to citation that is attached to this affidavit and marked as Exhibit B.

[or]

3 *[name of person served]* served on me the document referred to in Rule 25-11(4) *[set out whichever one of the following 3 choices is correct: (b)(i)/(b)(ii)/(b)(iii)(A)]* and has not, alone or with others, obtained a grant of probate.

SWORN (OR AFFIRMED)   )
BEFORE ME at *[location]*,   )
British Columbia,   )
on *[month, day, year]*   )
)
_____   )   _____
A commissioner for taking   )
affidavits for British Columbia   )
)

[print name or affix stamp of commissioner]

Form P35 (Rule 25-12(2))

No. *[specify]*
Registry *[specify]*

In the Supreme Court of British Columbia

In the Matter of the Estate of *[legal name of deceased]*, deceased

REQUISITION FOR SUBPOENA

[Rule 22-3 of the Supreme Court Civil Rules applies to all forms.]

Filed by: *[person(s)]*

Required: A subpoena requiring *[name]* to deliver to the registrar the following document(s): *[specify]*

1   This requisition for subpoena is filed under Rule 25-12(2).

2   Attached to this requisition for subpoena is a draft of the subpoena required.

3   The evidence in support of the application is *[specify]*. *[Describe the affidavit by reference to the name of the person who swore that affidavit and the date on which it was sworn, and file that affidavit with this requisition.]*

[Complete the following if the filing of this requisition starts a proceeding.]

This requisition for subpoena is filed by *[name]*, whose address for service is as follows:

[You must set out the street address of the address for service. One or both of a fax number and an email address may be given as additional addresses for service.]

Street address for service: *[specify]*

Fax number address for service (if any): *[specify]*

Email address for service (if any): *[specify]*

Telephone number: *[specify]*

Date: *[month, day, year]*.

_____

Signature of

[ ]   filing person(s)

[ ]   lawyer for filing person(s)

[type or print name]

The Heritage Trust Estate Administration Boot Camp

Form P37 (Rule 25-12(3))

[style of proceeding]

SUBPOENA

[Rule 22-3 of the Supreme Court Civil Rules applies to all forms.]

To: *[name and address]*

You are ordered to deliver to the probate registry at the courthouse at *[location]* the following: *[state documents to be delivered]*, within 14 days after service of this subpoena on you.

If any of the specified documents are not in your possession or control, you are, within the same time, to deliver to the above-noted probate registry whichever of the specified documents that are in your possession or control and to file in the above-noted probate registry an affidavit indicating which of the specified documents are not in your possession or control and setting out what knowledge you have respecting those documents.

Date: *[month, day, year]*.

_____
Registrar

WARNING: Failure to deliver the specified documents as required by this subpoena can result in your arrest and committal to prison WITHOUT DELIVERY TO YOU OF ANY FURTHER NOTICE OR DOCUMENT.

Chapter 4

Is the Will a Valid Will?

Introduction

The purpose of applying for probate of a will is to determine that it is the valid last will of the deceased. There are a number of things to consider when determining whether the will of the deceased is a valid will. WESA covers who can make a valid will and how to make a valid will starting at section 36:

36 (1) A person who is 16 years of age or older and who is mentally capable of doing so may make a will.

   (2) A will made by a person under 16 years of age is not valid.

37 (1) To be valid, a will must be

   (a) in writing,

   (b) signed at its end by the will-maker, or the signature at the end must be acknowledged by the will-maker as his or hers, in the presence of 2 or more witnesses present at the same time, and

   (c) signed by 2 or more of the witnesses in the presence of the will-maker.

   (2) A will that does not comply with subsection (1) is invalid unless

   (a) the court orders it to be effective as a will under section 58,

   (b) it is a will recognized as valid under section 80, or

   (c) it is valid under another provision of this Act.

Testamentary Capacity

A will can be attacked by anyone holding the sincere belief that the will-maker lacked testamentary capacity at the time they signed the will. This would mean that at the time of signing, the will-maker lacked the mental capacity to be able to make a will.

A person's capacity may vary over certain periods of time. A person may have capacity on one day and not on another. In these situations, it is essential to document how capacity was assessed and to retain these records as capacity may be questioned later on. A will-maker may be entirely lucid and have satisfactory capacity during the interview with their lawyer to provide instructions but may not test adequately on the day upon which they are to execute the estate plan, which would mean that the lawyer could not take their signature. The capacity assessment at the time of the execution (or signing) of the estate plan is what will hold the most importance.

The leading case on assessing testamentary capacity to prepare and execute a Last Will and Testament disposing of property is *Banks v Goodfellow,* (1870) LR 5 QB 549. Frequently cited is the following passage:

> It is essential to the exercise of such a power that a testator shall understand the nature of the act and its effects; shall understand the extent of the property of which he is disposing; shall be able to comprehend and appreciate the claims to which he ought to give effect; and with a view to the latter object, that no disorder of the mind shall poison his affections, pervert his sense of right, or prevent the exercise of his natural faculties— that no insane delusion shall influence his will in disposing of his property and being about a disposal of it which, if the mind had been sound, would not have been made.

As a guideline, in Ontario, the test for testamentary capacity grew into the following, as quoted from *Schwartz v Schwartz* (1970) 10 DLR (3d) (Ont. CA):

> A testator must be sufficiently clear in his understanding and memory to know, on his own, and in a general way:
>
> (1) The nature and extent of his property;
> (2) The persons who are the natural objects of his bounty;
> (3) The testamentary provisions he is making and, he must moreover be capable of;
> (4) Appreciating these factors in relation to each other; and
> (5) Forming an orderly desire as to the disposition of his property.

Below is some commentary about testamentary capacity that you might find useful if you are the subject of an application to challenge a will, or you think there might be reason for you to make an application to challenge the validity of a will.

Bull Estate v Bull, (2015 BCSC 136) is a recent British Columbia decision that reinforces the long-standing provisions of testamentary capacity. Some considerations when testing for testamentary capacity are the following:

- The test for testamentary capacity is not onerous;

- Sufficient mental capacity to make a will may exist despite the presence of cognitive deterioration;

- A will-maker may have sufficient mental capacity even if his or her ability to manage other aspects of their lives is impaired;

- Having imperfect or impaired memory will not negate testamentary capacity unless it is so severe as to leave no disposing memory;

- A disposing memory is one able to comprehend, of its own volition, the essential elements of will making, property, objects, just claims to consideration, revoking of disposition and the like;

- Testamentary capacity is a legal and not a medical question, and therefore medical opinions, though valuable, are not determinative of testamentary capacity;

- Simply leaving an estate in a manner that some think is unkind will not negate testamentary capacity; and

- A delusion is more than getting the facts wrong, a delusion is a persistent belief in facts that no rational person would hold to be true.

If the testamentary capacity of a person is in question, this may open up a will to be challenged. Some indications that testamentary capacity might be in issue are the following:

- Large departures from an earlier testamentary document;

- Suspicious circumstances;

- The possibility of undue influence;

- An illness or mental illness present at the time the will was prepared;

- Knowledge that the will-maker was on medications or drugs that could have altered their mental state;

- A will-maker who rushed into preparing the will on an urgent basis.

The lawyer who drafted the will may be called upon as a witness to testify as to their making and retention of notes regarding testamentary capacity and their experience with the circumstances with the will-maker at the material time.

Undue Influence

Undue influence can be found within any relationship where one person is in a position of control or power over the other. The influencer will often ingrain their own agenda into the mind of the influenced. This could be seen, and is sometimes referred to, as a form of brainwashing since the more susceptible person (often an aging parent or someone in a more modest position than the influencer) succumbs to the suggestions of the influencer. The influencer is vying for the influenced to adopt their wishes and, most often, the influencer has only their own motives or personal gain in mind.

This is a particularly common occurrence in estate planning matters with an aging population.

Diagnosing a relationship between an influencer and influenced is very nuanced and almost never black and white. There can be strong ambiguity when attempting to evaluate the situation, and oftentimes, the person drafting the will will be required to make a judgment call that considers risk and potential liability or possible estate litigation at some point down the road.

There is very rarely a smoking gun to indicate that undue influence is present. Identifying undue influence is centered around risk assessment: determining how likely and susceptible the influenced may be to the influencer and measuring that susceptibility with how much the influencer stands to gain from applying pressure on the influenced.

The influencer will often feel a sense of entitlement. They may have been looking after the influenced, or they may perceive that their sibling(s) (if they are already viewed as 'successful') do not need the money or assets to survive.

Unfortunately, it is very often the case that by the time the client/influenced gets to a law firm to plan their estate, the damage of influence has already been done. When they are issuing instructions to the lawyer, the influenced may already have reached a point where they truly believe that their own intentions are navigating the decisions. It is difficult to reverse this control if the influenced continues to remain under the same circumstances and there is perpetuation of the alienation. If the influenced is an older person, as is often the case in estate planning, they may not like or appreciate intervention – so a lawyer or anyone trying to get the influenced to see things from a different perspective is commonly met with an unfavourable reaction.

It may be of interest for you to determine whether a will-maker was the subject of undue influence if there is an application to challenge the will or if you believe an application should be made. There are a variety of signs that may indicate circumstances of undue influence. These include:

- Multiple charges being made to wills within short periods of time.

- A record which show drastic changes from one will to the next or large departures from previously expressed intentions.

- A history of "lawyer shopping" – if the will-maker tries to get their estate plan done by a lawyer who suspects that undue influence is present, that lawyer may refuse to be retained to act as counsel. The will-maker and the influencer may then hop from lawyer to lawyer to try to find someone that will draft it according to their demands.

- The will-maker's child/friend/relative/influencer:
  - Scheduling all the appointments on behalf of the influenced party;
  - Being (or attempting to be) highly involved in all aspects of the planning process, including:
    - gathering of documents,
    - speaking on behalf of the will-maker,
    - attending all appointments (whether in the room with the lawyer or sitting in the waiting room),
    - offering to assist in helping the will-maker with comprehension or coaching the will-maker (using leading sentences to illicit a specific response from the will-maker) and communicating those wishes to the lawyer/support staff,
      - \> this may also be the case if there is a language barrier and the will-maker needs a translation,
  - giving instructions regarding the will-maker's will to anyone in the office who will listen, including the receptionist or paralegals, and emphasizing the reasons why the will-maker may want to bring upon that change – a sense of entitlement in which they are trying to convince others.
  - Being aggressive, rude, and bullying support staff then exhibiting exactly the opposite behaviour when in front of or in contact with the drafting lawyer.

The Heritage Trust Estate Administration Boot Camp

- o Never leaving the will-maker/influenced alone – always by their side and rarely agreeable to leaving the client alone with the lawyer. It may seem as though the influenced is kept under lock and key. Sometimes the influencer may be within earshot of the meeting with the lawyer (this is something that can easily be remedied by ensuring that meetings between the lawyer and the will-maker are completely private).

- The will-maker exhibiting a sense of unwarranted urgency – perhaps brought on by a rash decision or as a reaction to a specific situation that compelled the will-maker to initiate a change to immediately re-evaluate their estate plan.

- The will-maker reiterating the instructions multiple times, using different forms of language to relay the same information – this may indicate that the will-maker was being coached by the influencer.

- The will-maker transferring all their assets into joint names with the right of survivorship.

- The will-maker rarely speaking when drafting the will (may just nod, shake head, or use one-word answers) and having a blank look instead of one that indicates comprehension.

- A history of police being called by other concerned parties, or social workers called to assess the relationship – there may be people who suspect that influence is present and who report it to whomever might take interest.

If there is reason to suspect that undue influence may have been a factor in preparing a will, there could be reason to challenge the validity of that will in court.

Curative Provisions

As per section 37(2) of WESA, there are ways to effectively 'cure' a will that might otherwise be invalid. This requires a separate application, generally done in addition to the application for probate, in order for the Court to recognize the will as valid before it is submitted to probate. While this application process is outside the scope of this handbook, section 58 of WESA is reproduced below to provide the parameters of the court curing a deficiency in a will:

58   (1)   In this section, "record" includes data that

(a)   is recorded or stored electronically,

(b)   can be read by a person, and

(c)   is capable of reproduction in a visible form.

(2) On application, the court may make an order under subsection (3) if the court determines that a record, document or writing or marking on a will or document represents

(a) the testamentary intentions of a deceased person,

(b) the intention of a deceased person to revoke, alter or revive a will or testamentary disposition of the deceased person, or

(c) the intention of a deceased person to revoke, alter or revive a testamentary disposition contained in a document other than a will.

(3) Even though the marking, revocation, alteration or revival of a will does not comply with this Act, the court may, as the circumstances require, order that a record or document or writing or marking on a will or document be fully effective as though it had been made

(a) as the will or part of the will of the deceased person, or

(b) as a revocation, alteration, or revival of a will of the deceased person, or

(c) as the testamentary intention of the deceased person.

(4) If an alteration to a will makes a word or provision illegible and the court is satisfied that the alteration was not made in accordance with this Act, the court may reinstate the original word or provision if there is evidence to establish what the original word or provision was.

When determining whether to "cure" a will, the court will consider whether the document represents a deliberate and final expression of the will-maker's testamentary intention.

Codicil & Outside Documents

A codicil can republish the will, as it confirms the will as a valid testamentary instrument. If there is a defective will but a valid codicil, the codicil can adopt the will and re-publish it.

Wills, on occasion, mention other unattested documents that are outside the will. For these documents to constitute part of the will, the document must be in existence when the will was executed and the will must refer to them as existing documents.

Chapter 5

Initial Responsibilities of the Personal Representative

Introduction

Once you have made the decision to take on the role of personal representative, whether that be as an executor, an administrator with will annexed, or an administrator without will annexed, there are a number of steps that need to be taken immediately. The flowchart below provides a visual representation of the steps that will need to be taken.

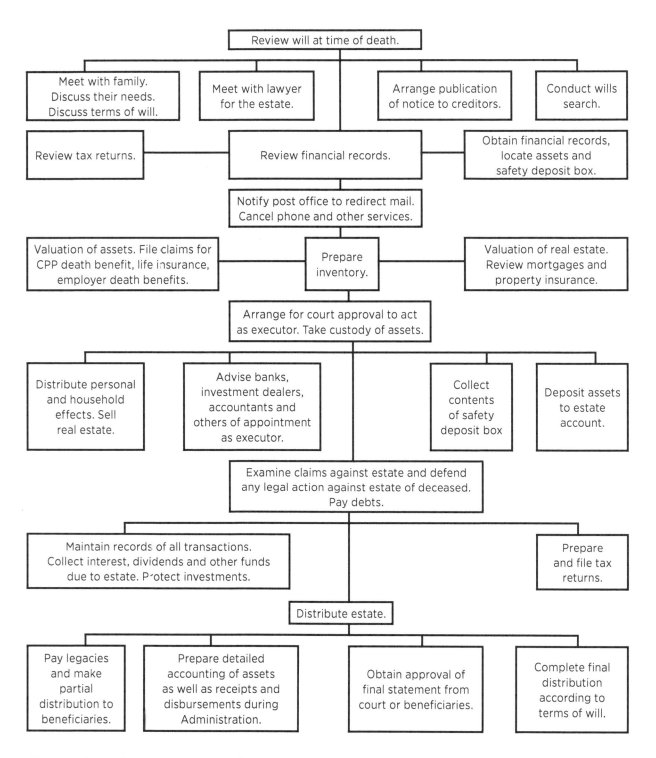

Arranging the Funeral and Dealing with the Remains

There are often directions contained within the will with respect to a funeral and to how the deceased wants their remains to be treated. If there are no directions contained within the will, the personal representative has the responsibility to make those decisions on behalf of the estate. They may want to consult with people close to the deceased to get an idea of what the deceased would have wanted but ultimately it remains the decision of the personal representative to make the final word.

The funeral home typically takes care of ordering and obtaining originals of the Certificate of Death from the Vital Statistics Agency, and they will charge the personal representative for these copies. Alternatively, you can order death certificates yourself by contacting the Vital Statistics Agency. Obtaining a death certificate is not limited to family, anyone can order one using the Vital Statistics Agency's website or by calling them. It is important to order multiple copies or at the very least have a lawyer or notary provide you with certified or notarial copies of the death certificate, as you will need to provide proof of death to various financial institutions or insurance agencies when dealing with the deceased's estate.

The *Cremation, Interment and Funeral Services Act* (SBC 2004, c 35), governs that the duty to dispose of the deceased's remains rests with the personal representative. If there is no executor, the statute allows for the married spouse or common law spouse to make the decision, or other relatives (adult children and then grandchildren) if there is no spouse. If the person with priority under the statute is unable or unwilling to act, the next person of priority is given the responsibility. If there is more than one person in the priority position, such as a deceased having no spouse but two or more adult children, and they cannot decide who will resume the responsibility, the governing law states that the priority goes to the eldest child first, then continues down the line.

Payment of the funeral expenses and disposing of the remains is a charge against the estate. It is usually appropriate for the executor or person arranging the funeral to make the payment directly from the deceased's bank account by going to the bank and producing the receipts for the costs to the bank for payment. Importantly, the receipts should show that the arrangements were "appropriate" and "reasonable", which does not necessarily cover all funeral expenses. The arrangements need to be proportional to the size of the estate and not overly lavish if the estate cannot afford such a funeral. Care and caution should be exercised when dealing with a small or insolvent estate as the executor or family member arranging the funeral may be called upon to cover any shortfall. Note that the person who provides instructions to the funeral home is the person who is responsible for paying all of the expenses incurred. The payor is entitled to be reimbursed from the estate in a higher priority than other creditors of the estate, as long as the expenses were reasonable.

Insolvent Estates

If you are administering an estate where there isn't enough money to pay the estate's debts, you will probably be dealing with disappointed creditors and beneficiaries and they might blame you. You should seek legal advice if this is the case.

Section 170 of WESA states that where there isn't enough money to pay all the estate's claims, the claims must be paid in a prescribed order:

1. Secured creditors

2. Funeral expenses

3. Executor's expenses

4. Wages to the deceased's employees

5. Claims for spousal support or child support

6. Municipal taxes

7. Rent payments to landlord

Locating the Will

It is the responsibility of the personal representative to look in all reasonable places to find the last will of the deceased. This may mean contacting the deceased's estate lawyer to search their vault, attending the deceased's bank to open and review the contents of the safety deposit box, searching through the deceased's filing cabinets or office, searching through the deceased's computer files, or going through the deceased's house carefully to see if there are any testamentary documents around that might express the deceased's last wishes. As noted in a previous chapter, because there are now curative provisions under WESA, any document may be construed as a testamentary intention so the will does not necessarily need to adhere to the strict provisions and formalities of a last will and testament. There is also the possibility that the deceased made codicils to the will or prepared memorandums that might have bequeathed personal items upon death.

To look in a safety deposit box, you will need to make an appointment at the bank to open the box of the deceased. You will need to bring the deposit box key and the original Certificate of Death, as well as your own identification. Identification requirements may vary depending on location; it is usually two pieces of government-issued ID, one with a photograph.

If you do not have the key, the safety deposit box may need to be drilled open. Depending on institution policies, they may not allow the box to be drilled open until an estate grant is obtained.

If you do have the key and the original will is in the box naming you as the executor, the bank will allow you to open the box to take the original will. At the same time, you and the representative from the financial institution will take a complete inventory of the safety deposit box so that any assets can be listed for the estate grant application later on. There may be certificates of securities, insurance policies, funeral contracts or cemetery plot deeds, bonds, jewellery, coins or other collections that might need valuation. You should take copies of the front and back of any bonds or securities, as you will not be allowed to go back into the safety deposit box until you have received the estate grant.

In addition to conducting your own personal search of the deceased's house and other places where they may have placed the will, it is mandatory to do a Wills Notice Search with the Vital Statistics Agency. When a person in British Columbia makes and executes a will, they have the ability to register a Wills Notice with Vital Statistics. The will-maker will advise the Vital Statistics Agency of the date they signed the will, the location of the will, and their personal identification information. It is important to note that the Vital Statistics Agency does not keep a copy of the will, they are only advised as to its particulars and location. Please note that while it is mandatory to search the Wills Notice registry upon the death of a person in British Columbia, it is not mandatory to file a Wills Notice in the first place; therefore, searching the Wills Notice registry does not guarantee that any Wills Notice found is the last will of the deceased.

To conduct a Wills Notice Search with Vital Statistics, you will need to have the information of the deceased including their full legal name (along with any aliases they may have gone by), their date and place of birth, and their date and place of death. You will need to retain the original search, whether it comes back with any results or not, and submit them with the rest of the estate grant application materials.

If the Wills Notice Search comes back with no results, indicating that no Wills Notice was ever filed with the Vital Statistics Agency, and you have found a will of the deceased then the will with the latest date in your possession will be considered to be the last will of the deceased. The absence of a Wills Notice does not invalidate any will.

The application for a Wills Notice Search can be obtained online at the Government of British Columbia website or at a Vital Statistics Agency office. Complete the form and submit it to the Vital Statistics Agency (either by mail or in person) with a photocopy of the death certificate and the appropriate payment. The Vital Statistics Agency will provide you with a Certificate of the Results of the Wills Notice Search. Keep this certificate for when you apply to the court for probate. In applying for probate, you need to provide the court with two copies of the certificate (Supreme Court Civil Rules, Rule 25-3(2)(c)).

You can choose to have the Certificate of the Results of the Wills Notice Search mailed to you or delivered by courier. If you wish to have the results mailed to you, the cost is $20 per will search, plus an additional $5 for each name (alias) that the will-maker may have used. The search results will be completed within 20 business days, plus the mailing time from Victoria to your mailing address. If you wish to have the results couriered to you, the cost will include an additional $33 for the courier fee. The results will be completed the next business day, plus the time it takes from the courier to deliver the results to you. Alternatively, if you have a BC Online account, you can conduct the Wills Notice Search entirely online with an original Certificate of the Results sent to you by mail. More information, plus the address of the Agency, can be found on the Government of BC's website.

A sample Application for Search of Wills Notice is included at the end of this chapter.

Reviewing the Will

As mentioned in the previous chapter, the executor must read and review the will, if such document exists, and determine whether there are any concerns regarding its validity. The will is also an instruction manual to delineate the executor's responsibilities and powers, and to guide the administration of the estate.

If the will was made in British Columbia, it must adhere to the legislative requirements of making a will, including that it must be signed at the end in the presence of two adult witnesses. See Chapter 4 with respect to the requirements of a valid will.

You will need to confirm that any gifts or appointments in the will have not been revoked. This could happen due to the end of a spousal relationship. A spousal relationship has terminated when a divorce order has been issued, or when there has been an event that causes an interest in family property to arise under the *Family Law Act,* such as a party commencing court proceedings for a division of family property. In the case of a common-law relationship, the relationship is terminated when one of the parties ends the relationship. You can find more information on this in Chapter 7. Remember from Chapter 1 that if the will-maker died before March 31, 2014, and they were married after making their will, then the will-maker's will is revoked on the marriage unless there was a contrary intention expressed in the will and it was made in contemplation of marriage. If the will-maker died after March 31, 2014, got married and then the will is not revoked.

A gift or appointment may also be found to be invalid. If you discover that the will has been witnessed by a beneficiary under the will, or the spouse of a beneficiary under the will, then the specific gift to this beneficiary is invalid. This will not invalidate the will, only that specific gift; however, there is now the ability to apply to the court to declare that the gift is valid if there was a clear intention that the deceased intended to make that gift despite the beneficiary being a witness. In this case, the personal representative would need to have the consent of all of the residuary beneficiaries or a court order.

You may unearth mistakes or ambiguities in the will that need to be corrected. With WESA, there is now the possibility to rectify these mistakes or ambiguities at the time of the application for the estate grant, under Section 59. The court may determine that the will does not fulfill the deceased's intentions, owing to some accidental slip or omission, or there might have been a misunderstanding of instructions or failure to follow the will-maker's instructions when the lawyer or notary drafted the will. Any application under Section 59 must be made within 180 days of the issuance of the estate grant, unless the court otherwise allows.

Safeguarding Assets

The personal representative is responsible for taking whatever steps necessary to safeguard estate assets, including taking possession of assets and papers that might otherwise go missing. A full and complete search of the deceased's residence and other places that might house important papers and other items is absolutely necessary to ensure that you are fulfilling your responsibilities.

Below is a list of suggested steps to properly safeguard estate assets. These suggestions apply to many estates, but they may not all apply to the estate that you are administering. This is not a complete list of assets; there may be other assets that require protection and that aren't dealt with below.

1. Search for cash, insurance policies, securities, jewellery, and other valuables and arrange for their safekeeping. Cancel the deceased's credit cards.

2. Lock up the deceased's residence if it is not occupied and dispose of any perishables. Advise the police if the property is not under proper supervision.

3. Arrange for an immediate inventory of all personal assets. You may consider removing any valuables from the deceased's home and placing them in secure storage if it is going to be left vacant. You should consider taking photographs of the valuables in case any dispute arises about their state later on. Special consideration should be used if the deceased owned any firearms. Check to ensure that they had the appropriate licenses for the firearms and whether they were registered. You will need to ensure their safekeeping. If there is no registration or license, you should contact the police on the non-emergency line to ask how to deal with the firearms.

4. Check the insurance on the deceased's assets (e.g., house, furniture, motor vehicle). Check the expiry dates and the vacancy provisions to ensure that the coverage continues (a 30-day vacancy limit applies in most policies insuring residential property). You should ensure that there is coverage for fire, vandalism, and liability insurance. Notify the insurers of the death. You should be sure that there is adequate property insurance to cover the current value of the real estate and all of the household effects.

5. Review the insurance policy on the vehicle and if it permits use. Note that if a vehicle is used without proper insurance, the personal representative of the estate

may become personally liable. It may be more appropriate to purchase storage insurance until the estate grant is obtained and the insurance is ready to be transferred to the name of the personal representative or to a beneficiary.

6. Arrange for interim management of the deceased's business.

7. Collect and deposit any outstanding cheques (e.g., pensions, dividends, interest, salary).

8. Redirect mail if necessary. It is usually prudent to sign up for one year of service in case there are any bills or mail that is delivered quarterly or annually. The personal representative can arrange this by going to Canada Post with the Certificate of Death and proof of their appointment as personal representative such as the estate grant or a copy of the will, and providing photo identification.

9. Check for mortgages (and determine if they are life-insured) and agreements for sale and make the payments to keep them up to date.

10. Check leases and tenancies. Give tenants notice about where to send rent payments and give notice of termination if necessary.

11. Review the last cheques written by the deceased to ensure that there were no irregularities.

12. Apply for Canada Pension Plan Death Benefits. If you need any information, you can contact them at 1-800-277-9914. If you are mailing any documents to Canada Pension, the address is: PO Box 1177, Federal Building, Victoria, BC, V7W 2V2.

13. Contact and notify any financial institutions, such as banks, credit unions, and trust companies of the death. You may need to provide written authorization as the personal representative and send a copy of the will or death certificate, depending on the policies of the financial institutions. You should review any bank statements (paper or online) in the deceased's name to see if they held accounts at any specific institution.

14. There may also be dormant or unclaimed bank accounts which you can search for at the Bank of Canada, which may have unclaimed balances if a bank account has not been used for ten years or more.

15. If the deceased had minor children, the will should contain a clause regarding their wishes in terms of guardianship. The personal representative is responsible for ensuring the safety of any minor or dependent children. If there is no will, the administrator needs to locate the nearest next of kin to take care of any minor or dependent children and that next of kin will need to apply to the court to become the lawful guardian. Any disputes of the guardianship of the children will be decided by the court.

16. The deceased may have had pets that may or may not have been included in their will. They may need to be placed in the care of a family member or friend, or a kennel or boarding place.

17. Cancel accounts and notify certain organizations of the death, including:

   a. Passport Canada;

   b. Social Insurance Number at Service Canada;

   c. Medical Services Plan;

   d. Credit bureaus; and

   e. Utilities and other services (such as cable, internet, heat, hydro, water, phone, subscriptions, reward programs, and credit cards).

Gathering Information

In order to fill out the estate grant application forms completely, you will need key pieces of information. You will need information such as full legal names, the last known address of the deceased, citizenship, date and place of death, relevant documents, asset and liability information, and names and addresses of beneficiaries and intestate successors.

We have included a client intake form at the end of this chapter that may assist in compiling the necessary information.

Listing Assets and Liabilities

Part of the estate grant application includes an affidavit that lists the assets and liabilities of the estate as of the date of death. The Affidavit of Assets and Liabilities is filed using Form P10. This inventory will be used to determine probate fees, taxes, and the eventual distribution of the estate, and is very important to have completely accurate and inclusive.

Below is a list of suggested steps to determine and list estate assets and liabilities. These suggestions apply to many estates, but they may not all apply to the estate that you are administering.

1. Arrange with the deceased's bank to view and list the contents of the safety deposit box.

2. Record all the expenses you incur in doing your job as executor, including funeral expenses.

3. List all the banks where the deceased had accounts or loans. Include the account numbers. For each account, **request the balance and the interest accrued to the date of death.** Collect any bank books or statements of account and have them

posted up to the date of death. Note that accounts may include term deposits, Registered Retirement Savings Plans, and Registered Retirement Income Funds.

4. List all securities, stocks, or bonds owned by the deceased. Obtain the market value at the date of death.

5. Search the Land Title Registry in the provinces where the deceased held any property. List all real estate which the deceased owned alone or with others. Also list any mortgages or agreements for sale that the deceased held or owed. Provide the full addresses of all properties. Have appraisals done, as of the date of death, on any properties that were not jointly owned.

6. List all estate income that will be received after the date of death. This may include cheques that have not been received or deposited from pensions, deferred profit-sharing plans, dividends, interest, salary, or any repayments or refunds due to the deceased.

7. List any business assets or shares in any company owned by the deceased. Obtain appropriate valuations.

8. Identify all people and businesses who owed money to the deceased. Provide any details you can of the nature of the debt and the amount owing.

9. Run a search of the Personal Property Security Registry for any outstanding registrations. List any other assets, including cars, boats, household goods, jewellery, cameras, and other personal effects. Provide descriptions, including serial numbers if possible. Include estimated values.

10. List all outstanding debts and liabilities of the deceased.

11. List any agreements or court orders to which the deceased was a party or under which the deceased was liable. This might include divorce decrees, maintenance orders, marriage agreements, Family Law Act orders, guarantees, buy-sell agreements, partnership agreements, leases, employment contracts, and insurance owned by the deceased on the life of another.

12. Search for any digital assets, like bitcoin, iTunes, domain names and/or loyalty programs.

13. Review previously filed tax returns to discover any other sources of income that may lead you to discover further assets you may not be aware of.

When you have your listing of assets and liabilities, note the way in which each one was held by the deceased. Assets and liabilities may be held jointly (in joint tenancy or as tenants in common) or in trust for another person, or there may be a designated beneficiary. Finding out how the assets or liabilities are held will be determinative as to whether they are included in the Statement of Assets and Liabilities when you apply for the estate grant. For example, if an RRSP was held by the deceased and has a designated beneficiary, the entire account would pass outside of the estate and be transferred to the beneficiary and it would not be counted towards the calculation of probate fees. Or, if a piece of real property was held in joint tenancy sometimes the whole of the property will automatically be transferred to the surviving joint tenant.

In transferring assets and estimating the value of the estate it may be necessary to find out the fair market value of individual assets. There are various methods of valuation, depending on the asset:

- For household goods, an auctioneer may make an informal and cursory appraisal and conduct an estate auction, leaving the profit for the estate.

- In valuing investments for tax purposes, you need to calculate the capital gain (the amount it is worth at the time of death, less the initial purchase cost). It may be necessary to hire an accountant.

- If the assets include jewellery, antiques or collectibles, or other assets for which the value is uncertain, you may need to get a professional appraisal.

- For valuation of estates involving overseas assets or business assets, you will likely need to hire an accountant.

In some circumstances it may be difficult to ascertain the value of the property, such as with private company shares, pensions, or jewellery. It may become prudent for you to retain the services of an appraiser, accountant, or other professional. For real property, sometimes it is appropriate to use the BC Property Assessment for the year of death, and other times it may be better to obtain a formal appraisal or a market evaluation from a real estate agent.

Sometimes financial institutions are not forthcoming with information about the deceased's holdings, especially if you are applying as an administrator and have not been appointed under a will. In these circumstances, it is possible under WESA to file the entire estate grant application package without the Statement of Assets and Liabilities and instead obtain what is referred to as an Authorization to Obtain Estate Information. This is a document issued by the court registry that can be provided to any financial institution who will then be obligated to provide you with the information requested within 30 days of being served with the Authorization. Note that under the previous legislation it was possible to put a value on a Statement of Assets and Liabilities as "To be determined". It is no longer acceptable to indicate this on the statement except under very limited circumstances. If you do not have the balances as of the date of death, you will need to apply to obtain the Authorization to Obtain Estate Information to ensure complete accuracy in your statement.

Identifying the Beneficiaries and Intestate Successors of the Estate

It is important to uncover all the beneficiaries under the will and/or the intestate successors (those who have a right or interest to inherit the estate where there is no will) at the start in order to determine who you will need to report to, who you have a fiduciary duty to, and who you might need to be concerned about if someone decides to challenge the will. You will need to identify the following beneficiaries, if applicable:

Spouse *
Anyone that the deceased was or had ever been married to, as well as anyone with whom the deceased ever had a common-law relationship. For each, note the full legal name, address, details about the relationship, (e.g., date of marriage, date of divorce, date of death if applicable), and any other relevant information.

Children *
All the deceased's children, whether they were born inside or outside of marriage. For each, note the full legal name and address.

Beneficiaries
Each beneficiary named in the will who is not already listed as a spouse or child. For each, note the full name, address, and relationship to the deceased.

Intestate Successors
Each person (other than those already listed above) who would be entitled to the estate if there were no will. If the deceased had no living spouse, child, grandchild, or parents, for example, then you should include the deceased's brothers, sisters, nieces and nephews. For each, note the names and addresses.

Guardian(s)
If any person that you have listed above is under age 19, you must include that person's birthdate, and the names and address of that person's parents and/or legal guardians. If only one parent or guardian is responsible for the minor, only that parent's name and address is required.

*See Chapter 7 for more information on the WESA definition of "Spouse" and "Children".

Ongoing Obligation to Maintain Accounts and Expenses

Because you are under a constant responsibility to account to beneficiaries, it is extremely important to keep a running tally of all estate expenses and to monitor the estate assets and liabilities. Your records should include the full particulars of any expenses that you incurred personally or paid out of estate funds. Again, keeping the appropriate receipts could save you a lot of grief if there are any disputes as to the expenses. You should also keep a log of all the time you spend working on the estate to show how many hours you logged in relation to your position as the personal representative. This may warrant you obtaining higher compensation if it was a particularly difficult estate.

You have a duty to keep proper and complete records. At the end of the estate, you will need to account to the beneficiaries for your administration of the entire estate. These accounts will need to be approved before you can claim any compensation for acting as a personal representative.

Income Taxes

As the personal representative, you must file certain income tax returns for the deceased and the estate. The basic tax filing obligations are as follows:

1. You must file a T1 (General) return for any year before the year of death if the deceased had not filed a return for that year and if tax is payable. Any late or unfiled returns must be filed as soon as possible. With respect to the prior year's return where the deceased died before the normal filing deadline, the return must be filed by six months from the deceased's date of death or the normal filing deadline, whichever is later.

2. You must file a T1 (General) return for the year of death (January 1 to the date of death), in most circumstances. The return must be filed either six months from the date of death or by April 30 of the year following the year of death [June 15 if the deceased taxpayer carried on a business as a proprietor or a partner in the year of death], whichever is later. It is best practice to arrange for this return to be filed as early as possible so that you can obtain a Clearance Certificate (explained in Chapter 11) from the Canada Revenue Agency.

3. You must file a T3 return within 90 days of each fiscal period of the estate. For 2016 and later tax years, a graduated rate estate (GRE) can have a non-calendar tax year (the period for which the accounts of the estate are made up for purposes of assessment). A GRE will have a deemed tax year-end on the day on which the estate stops being a GRE, which will be no later than the day on which the 36-month period after the death of the individual ends. Later tax year-ends will generally be on a calendar-year basis.

Depending on the nature of the deceased's income, the estate may be allowed to file other income tax returns, and it may be desirable for you to do so.

It is recommended that you retain an accountant to assist in preparing income tax returns.

This form is fillable. Click in Surname field to begin.

Vital Statistics Agency — BRITISH COLUMBIA

[Clear form] [Print]

APPLICATION FOR SEARCH
OF WILLS NOTICE

APPLICANT'S INFORMATION	FOR OFFICE USE ONLY

APPLICANT'S INFORMATION

Surname	Given Name(s)

FOR OFFICE USE ONLY

APPLICATION FOR SERVICE NUMBER

Mailing Address

Relationship to the Subject of the Will Search

City/Town/Village, Province/State, Country | Postal/Zip Code

Home Phone Number (include area code)

If Company, Attention

Work Phone Number (include area code)

Is this application a Wills Search for a *living person*? (See 2c under "Procedure" on back of page.) ❏ Yes ❏ No

Complete either Section A **or** Section B, then complete Section C

SECTION A - APPLICATION FOR WILLS SEARCH	SECTION B - SOLICITORS OR NOTARIES ONLY

SECTION A - APPLICATION FOR WILLS SEARCH

❏ A photocopy of a government-issued certificate of death is enclosed.

X _____
Signature of Applicant

SECTION B - SOLICITORS OR NOTARIES ONLY

I, _____ am:

❏ (a) a solicitor of the Supreme Court of British Columbia

❏ (b) a member of the Society of Notaries Public of British Columbia

❏ 1) acting on behalf of the below listed individual I request a Living Will Search

OR

❏ 2) after due investigation, I believe the below named individual,

died on _____

at _____

X _____
Signature of Solicitor/Notary Acting in accordance with the prescribed legislation

SECTION C - SEARCH REQUEST DETAILS OF DECEASED PERSON

	FEE
Date of birth _____ Place of birth _____	
Full name (**SURNAME**, Given Names) _____	$ 20.00
Also known as (**SURNAME**, Given Names) _____	+ $ 5.00
Also known as (**SURNAME**, Given Names) _____	+ $ 5.00
Also known as (**SURNAME**, Given Names) _____	+ $ 5.00
Also known as (**SURNAME**, Given Names) _____	+ $ 5.00
Also known as (**SURNAME**, Given Names) _____	+ $ 5.00
Also known as (**SURNAME**, Given Names) _____	+ $ 5.00
Also known as (**SURNAME**, Given Names) _____	+ $ 5.00
Courier Service* Requested ❏ Yes ❏ No _____	+ $ 33.00

*NOTE: All services, other than courier services, are mailed. Courier service requests are produced the next business day. Delivery time is dependent on shipping destination. Fee includes the cost of the search of our records. Search results are generated upon confirmation of a record held. If no record of the event is found, the fee is applied to the search process. Courier service is not attempted at the following residence types: post office box, apartment complex, homes that use Super Box (community) mailboxes and basement suites. Instead, a delivery notice with instructions is left at those residences and the package delivered to the nearest postal outlet. ID and signature are required upon pick up.

TOTAL: $ _____

PAYMENT METHODS

❏ Cheque' ❏ Money Order' ❏ Visa ❏ MasterCard ❏ American Express

Amount Enclosed: $ _____

Interac/Cash payment may be made in person at any Service BC office. 'If paying by cheque or money order, make payable to the **Minister of Finance**. Postdated cheques are not accepted.

X _____
Card holder signature

_____
PRINT card holder name as shown on credit card

Credit Card # _____ Expiry date _____

Note: Credit card information is not retained. Upon authorization of the payment request, all credit card information is destroyed.

VSA 532 2018/12/12

[Clear Form] [Print]

Please read notes on page 2 of this form.

APPLICATION FOR SEARCH OF WILLS NOTICE

- This form may be utilized to determine if the deceased person filed a Wills Notice with the Vital Statistics Agency indicating the location of their will.

- A wills search can be a required component of the wills probate process within the Province of British Columbia. Details of the full probate process are available from your nearest Probate Court.

PROCEDURE

1. Please complete the front side of this form in full.

    a) Include your postal code in the mailing address information to ensure search results can be successfully returned to you.

    b) Provide a telephone number in case your search result is returned as undeliverable.

    c) Before an application can be processed, it must be signed by the applicant in the location provided on the front side of this form.

    Note: The Application for Search of Wills Notice form <u>must</u> be signed by the applicant prior to probate submission.

2. Eligibility

    a) Provide a **photocopy of a government-issued certificate of death. Note**: A signed statement is only accepted *under rare circumstances*. Contact the Vital Statistics Agency for further information.

    b) A lawyer or notary may apply either by acting on behalf of the subject of the wills search or by stating that the subject has passed away.

    c) Other than a lawyer or a notary, only the individual themselves may apply for a wills search for a living person. You will be required to provide picture identification in descending order of preference:

        - Driver's Licence
        - Passport
        - BC ID Card

    You must clearly indicate "Will Search for a Living Person" on the first page of the application.

3. Please provide details about the deceased person to ensure the correct Wills Notice information can be located.

    a) The birthdate (month, day, year - example: April 15, 1915).

    b) Place of birth.

    c) The full name of the deceased person (example: SIMPSON, WILLIAM WALTER).

    d) In those instances where a deceased person may have used another name and may have filed other legal documents under that name, use the "also known as" line(s). **Note: There is an extra charge for this/these additional search(es)**.

    Example: SIMPSON, WILLIAM WALTER also known as SIMPSON, BILL
    Example: PETERS, MARY LOUISE also known as KERR, MARY LOUISE

4. Mail your application for Wills Notice Search to the Vital Statistics Agency, or visit a Service BC office for in-person services. For Service BC locations, go to www.servicebc.gov.bc.ca.

ESTIMATED TIME OF DELIVERY

Mail: Results are produced within 20 business days; add mailing time *from Victoria* to you.

Courier: Results are produced the next business day; add courier delivery time *from Victoria* to you.

CONTACT INFORMATION

Mailing Address: Vital Statistics Agency, PO Box 9657 Stn Prov Govt, Victoria BC V8W 9P3
Telephone: 250 952-2681 (Victoria & Outside B.C.), 1 888 876-1633 (within B.C.)
Web: www2.gov.bc.ca/gov/content/life-events

Apply for services in person at any Service BC Centre. Visit www.servicebc.gov.bc.ca for your nearest location.

This information is collected by the Vital Statistics Agency under section 26(c) of the *Freedom of Information and Protection of Privacy Act*, and will be used to fulfil the requirements of the *Vital Statistics Act* for the release of Last Will and Testament information. Should you have any questions about the collection of this personal information, please contact: Manager, Vital Statistics Agency, 250 952-2681, PO Box 9657, Stn Prov Govt, Victoria BC V8W 9P3

Estate Administration Information

Estate of:		
Personal Representative:		Date:
Address:	Tel. No.	Home:
		Work:
Deceased left a: Will ☐ No Will ☐	E-mail:	

A. DECEASED'S VITAL STATISTICS AND BACKGROUND INFORMATION

Legal name of deceased:	
Any aliases:	
Last address:	
Date and place of birth:	
Date and place of death:	
Cause of death:	
Length of last illness:	
Social insurance No.	
Province where deceased ordinarily resided:	
Occupation/Job Title:	
Name and address of employer:	
Death benefits or pension:	
Name and address of funeral home:	

Accountant(s)
    Name
    Address
    Contact person	

Last income tax return filed for:	

B. DECEASED'S MARITAL STATUS

Marital status:	
Name of spouse: Including common-law spouse	
Spouse's SIN No.:	
Address of spouse:	
Spouse's date and place of birth:	
Date and place of marriage: (or when cohabitation started)	
Maiden (or previous) name of spouse:	
If widowed, spouse's date and place of death:	
Marriage contract: N.A. ☐	

C. NEXT OF KIN
(set out the Deceased's family tree)

Note: If any next of kin are under 19 years, include names and address of Parents/Guardians.

Name:	Date of Birth:	
Address:	Tel: H W	
	Relationship to Deceased:	
Name:	Date of Birth:	
Address:	Tel: H W	
	Relationship to Deceased:	
Name:	Date of Birth:	
Address:	Tel: H W	
	Relationship to Deceased:	
Name:	Date of Birth:	
Address:	Tel: H W	
	Relationship to Deceased:	

Did any deceased children leave children or spouse who have survived the Deceased? Yes ☐ No ☐

D. BENEFICIARIES UNDER THE WILL
(include all contingent beneficiaries)

Notes: If a beneficiary is under 19 years, include names and addresses of Parents/Guardians. If the beneficiary is or may be a mentally disordered person or has a representative or a committee, include the name and address of such representative or committee.

Name:	Date of Birth:
Address:	Tel: H W
	Relationship to Deceased:
Name:	Date of Birth:
Address:	Tel: H W
	Relationship to Deceased:
Name:	Date of Birth:
Address:	Tel: H W
	Relationship to Deceased:
Name:	Date of Birth:
Address:	Tel: H W
	Relationship to Deceased:
Name:	Date of Birth:
Address:	Tel: H W
	Relationship to Deceased:
Name:	Date of Birth:
Address:	Tel: H W
	Relationship to Deceased:

E.   TESTAMENTARY DOCUMENTS

Date of Will:	**Location of Will**:
Codicil: N.A. ☐ or date:	**Location of Codicil**:
Execution: Are witnesses beneficiaries or spouses of beneficiaries: Yes ☐ No ☐	
Any other testamentary documents (e.g., memorandum referred to in the Will) Yes ☐ No ☐	
If yes: Describe:	

F.   PERSONAL REPRESENTATIVES

If Executor, intending to Apply?: Yes ☐ No ☐		If Administrator: Bondable Yes ☐ No ☐	
Representative's Name:			
Relationship to Deceased:			
Address:		Tel: Home	
		Work	
Occupation:		Citizenship:	
S.I.N.		Date of Birth:	
If Executor, intending to Apply?: Yes ☐ No ☐		If Administrator: Bondable Yes ☐ No ☐	
Name:			
Relationship to Deceased:			
Address:		Tel: Home	
		Work	
Occupation:		Citizenship:	
S.I.N.		Date of Birth:	
If Executor, intending to Apply?: Yes ☐ No ☐		If Administrator: Bondable Yes ☐ No ☐	
Name:			
Relationship to Deceased:			
Address:		Tel: Home	
		Work	
Occupation:		Citizenship:	
S.I.N.		Date of Birth:	

G.   ASSETS

1.   REAL ESTATE   N.A. ☐

Street Address	Legal description (If known)	Market Value	Mortgage approx. outstanding(**)	Interest (e.g. Joint Tenancy)	Nature (*)

(*)   **(residential, recreational or investment)**
(**)   **Is mortgage life insured?**

2.   MORTGAGES, AGREEMENTS FOR SALE

Property address and legal description: _____

_____

_____

Mortgagor/Purchaser: _____

Balance owing: $ _____

3.   SECURITIES, BONDS, SHARES

Name, address and telephone number of broker: _____

_____

Describe shares (on attached list if insufficient space) _____

_____

_____

4. CASH ON HAND (including uncashed cheques, salary, Old Age Pension, etc.)

_____

_____

5. BANK ACCOUNTS (including accounts held jointly with another person)

Bank:	Name(s) on Account	Type & Account No.
Address:		
Safety deposit box: Yes ☐ No. ☐		
Bank:	**Name(s) on Account**	**Type & Account No.**
Address:		
Safety deposit box: Yes ☐ No. ☐		
Bank:	**Name(s) on account**	**Type & Account No.**
Address:		
Safety deposit box: Yes ☐ No. ☐		

6. LIFE INSURANCE POLICIES

Name of Company:	Policy No.
Address:	Amount:
Designated beneficiary:	
Name of Company:	Policy No.
Address:	Amount:
Designated beneficiary:	

7. PENSIONS

Canada Pension: Yes ☐ No ☐

Other pensions: N.A. ☐ or list pensions:

8. OTHER BUSINESS INTERESTS (attach schedule if necessary)

(List interests in any business, e.g. sole proprietorship, partnership, private company)

Name:

_____

Value:

_____

Accountants:

_____

9. AUTOMOBILES

Year	Model	Serial Number	Value	Ownership:
				Joint ☐ Individual ☐
				Joint ☐ Individual ☐

10. OTHER PERSONAL PROPERTY (household effects and other – describe)

_____

_____

Listing or valuation/appraisal required: Yes: ☐ No: ☐

11. DEBTS, EXPENSES, AND LIABILITIES

CREDITORS			
Creditor – Name and Address	**Amount**	**Paid**	**Unpaid**
Funeral Home: Name: Address:	$	☐	☐
		☐	☐
		☐	☐

Chapter 6

Is an Estate Grant Necessary?

An estate grant is commonly known as a grant of probate. A court or registrar will make a grant (sometimes also called an estate grant or a representation grant) naming a person who is responsible for winding up the estate, paying the deceased's debts, and distributing the deceased's assets. If there is a will, the grant is a grant of probate and the person named to represent the deceased is the executor.

When a person dies, their assets may be:

1. Transferred to designated beneficiaries under life insurance policies or registered accounts such as RRSPs or RRIFs. The assets contained in those policies pass outside of the estate and are therefore not subject to probate fees and do not need to be listed on the Statement of Assets and Liabilities.

2. Transferred through a right of survivorship, such as a jointly held bank account or real property (a family home or vehicle).

3. Transferred to beneficiaries without a grant if there is a will and it is a very small estate. There is no minimum net worth for probate. Some institutions may transfer small accounts to a beneficiary if a threshold amount is met, for instance, if it is under $5,000. The amount varies from institution to institution and even from branch to branch, so you will need to determine this on your own. Note that ICBC can transfer a vehicle without a grant of probate if the estate is valued under $25,000. Additionally, if the estate's value is under $25,000, no probate fees will be payable to the probate registry if an estate grant is still required.

4. Passed to the personal representative under an estate grant.

An estate grant will be required when the deceased's assets are held solely and do not pass under beneficiary designation or by right of survivorship, and when the asset holder requires the grant to release the asset(s) to the personal representative. In this case, a person must be appointed by the Supreme Court of British Columbia to administer the assets of the estate. Until the estate grant is issued by the Court, the assets cannot be distributed by the personal representative.

Note that when there is no will, an estate grant will be required in all cases, unless the entire estate falls under section (1) or (2) above. If there is a will, it is not always necessary to obtain a grant of probate, since the authority of the executor is empowered by the will and not from a grant of probate.

Chapter 7

It's All in the Family

Introduction

It is important to familiarize yourself with the definition of spouses and children under the new WESA regime. WESA provides specific rules to determine whether someone qualifies as a spouse or a child. For further explanation of other next-of-kin, see Chapter 9 for the chart of Parentelic Distribution.

Definition of a Spouse

Part 2, Division 1, Section 2 dictates the meaning of a spouse under WESA:

2 (1) Unless subsection (2) applies, 2 persons are spouses of each other for the purposes of this Act if they were both alive immediately before a relevant time and

    (a) they were married to each other, or

    (b) they had lived with each other in a marriage-like relationship for at least 2 years.

  (2) Two persons cease being spouses of each other for the purposes of this Act if,

    (a) in the case of a marriage, an event occurs that causes an interest in family property, as defined in Part 5 of the *Family Law Act,* to arise, or

    (b) in the case of a marriage-like relationship, one or both persons terminate the relationship.

(2.1) For the purposes of this Act, spouses are not considered to have separated if, within one year after separation,

(a) they begin to live together again and the primary purpose for doing so is to reconcile, and

(b) they continue to live together for one or more periods, totaling at least 90 days.

(3) A relevant time for the purposes of subsection (1) is the date of death of one of the persons unless this Act specifies another time as the relevant time.

Children

There is no difference in the law if a child was born outside marriage. Any child born out of wedlock has the same status as a child that was born within a marriage.

If a child has been adopted, they essentially terminate the relationship with their birth parent (pre-adoption parent). The only way an adopted child will be entitled to the estate of their birth parent is if the birth parent has made some provision in their will for the child. The same goes for the pre-adoptive parent: they will not be entitled to any share of the estate of the child that has been adopted unless the child has made provision for them in their will. The only exception occurs if a child has been adopted by the spouse of the pre-adoptive birth parent, then there is no termination of the relationship of parent and child between the natural parent and the child with respect to succession rights.

If someone has a stepchild but they have not taken the steps to legally adopt the child, that child will not inherit from the stepparent on intestacy.

Chapter 8

Where There's a Will... There's a Way

Introduction

Now that you have gathered the appropriate information, reviewed the will, and chosen to proceed with becoming the executor of the estate, you need to start the application process.

In order to implement the large-scale changes brought about by WESA, the Supreme Court Civil Rules also required amendment. Section 25 of the rules were introduced.

The application for an estate grant is now governed by Rule 25-3. A standard (simple) application for a grant of probate will include the following prescribed forms:

P1—Notice of proposed application in relation to estate;
P2—Submission for estate grant;
P3/P4—Affidavit of application for grant of probate;
P9—Affidavit of delivery;
P10—Affidavit of assets and liabilities for domiciled estate grant.

In addition, an application for estate grant should include the original will and the results of the Search for Wills Notice issued by the Vital Statistics Agency, in duplicate, and possibly a letter from the Public Guardian and Trustee if required.

You may find it helpful to have a checklist of all the steps to take during the course of the estate administration. Included at the end of this chapter is a pre-grant estate administration checklist.

Form P1 Notice of Proposed Application in Relation to Estate

With the introduction of WESA into provincial law, the notice requirements shifted noticeably. The executor must figure out who is entitled to notice in accordance with section 121 of WESA, which states:

121 (1) An applicant for a grant of probate or administration must give notice of the proposed application to the persons referred to in the Supreme Court Civil Rules.

(2) An applicant or personal representative who, in accordance with the Supreme Court Civil Rules, makes reasonable efforts to discover the existence, identity or whereabouts of persons to whom the notice under subsection (1) is required to be given, but is unsuccessful, is not liable for any loss or damage arising from not giving the required notice except for claims to recover property or enforce an order under Division 6 of Part 4.

Section 25-2 of the Supreme Court Civil Rules expresses who is entitled to notice:

(1) Subject to this rule, unless the court otherwise orders, a person intending to apply for an estate grant or for the resealing of a foreign grant in relation to this estate of a deceased must, at least 21 days before submitting for filing the materials required for that application under this Part, deliver the following to the persons referred to in subrule (2):

a. **A notice that complies with subrule (3);**

b. **Whichever of the following, if any, that applies to the intended application:**

i. **If the intended applicant intends to apply for a grant of probate or a grant of administration with will annexed, a copy of the will in relation to which the application is to be made;**

ii. **If the intended applicant intends to apply for the resealing of a foreign grant or for an ancillary grant of probate or an ancillary grant of administration with will annexed, a copy of the foreign grant and, if the copy of the will in relation to which the foreign grant was issued is not attached to the foreign grant, a copy of the will;**

iii. **If the intended applicant intends to apply for an ancillary grant of administration without will annexed, a copy of the foreign grant.**

(2) The documents referred to in subrule (1) must be delivered to the following persons:

a. **If the deceased left a will, each of the following who is not a person by whom or on whose behalf the documents referred to in subrule (1) are to be delivered (a person by whom or on whose behalf the documents referred to in subrule (1) are to be delivered is, in this subrule, called an "intended applicant"):**

i. **Each person**

    A. **Who is named in the will as executor or alternate executor,**

    B. **Whose right to make an application for an estate grant in relation to the deceased is prior to or equal to the intended applicant's right to make that application, and**

    C. **Who is alive at the time of the deceased's death;**

ii. **Each beneficiary under the will who is not referred to in subparagraph (i) of this paragraph;**

iii. **Each person who, under Division 1 of Part 3 of the *Wills, Estates and Succession Act,* would have been an intestate successor if the deceased did not leave a will and who is not referred to in subparagraph (i) or (ii) of this paragraph;**

b. If the deceased did not leave a will,

    i. Each person who, under Division 1 of Part 3 of the *Wills, Estates and Succession Act,* is an intestate successor of the deceased, and

    ii. Each creditor of the deceased whose claim exceeds $10,000 and who is not referred to in subparagraph (i) of this paragraph;

c. If the deceased was a Nisga'a citizen, the Nisga'a Lisims government;

d. If the deceased was a member of a treaty first nation, the treaty first nation;

e. Any other person who, by court order under subrule (14)(a) is to receive notice;

f. Any person not referred to in paragraph (a), (b), (c), (d) or (e) of this subrule who has served a citation on the intended applicant in relation to the deceased.

(Emphasis added)

All of the appropriate people need to be mailed the P1 Notice and a copy of the will, if applicable. As a general rule, this includes all the beneficiaries, as well as the intestate successors (the people who would have a right to receive from the estate if there were no will – see Chapter 9 for an explanation of intestate successors). The reason that the intestate successors will receive notice is because there may be some reason that the will of the deceased turns out to be invalid, in which case, the deceased would have died without a will. If there are charities listed in the will as beneficiaries, then those charities need to be provided with Notice and the will as well. It is best practice to wait until you have received the results of the Search for a Wills Notice before you send out any notices to anyone, in case a later will is found.

There is the option to deliver the P1 Notice and copy of the will by email or fax; however, it is best practice to send it by regular mail. The reason for this is, if you send the package electronically, the court will require the recipient to acknowledge (usually by return email) that they have received it. The personal representative must then retain the email acknowledgement of the delivery of the notice until they are discharged as executor. If the person being provided with the notice does not acknowledge delivery, the personal representative will need to mail the notice and a copy of the will to them regardless; therefore, it is easier to mail it in first instance. The package is deemed "delivered" on the date that it is mailed. You will eventually need to swear an affidavit that will be filed with the estate grant application package attesting to mailing the P1 Notice and copy of the will, the date it was mailed on, and who it was mailed to.

It is important to note the date of mailing, as the personal representative must wait 21 days after mailing the Notice and the will before they will be allowed to file the rest of the estate grant application package to the Probate Registry. This 21-day waiting period allows anyone that received notice of the proposed application the opportunity to oppose the application, which they can do by filing a Notice of Dispute.

There are some common issues that may arise when delivering the P1 Notice:

Minors
Delivery must be made to the minor's parents – if the minor lives with all parents – or to the parent or guardian who has the responsibility for financial decisions relating to the minor. Otherwise, the notice should be delivered to each of the addresses where the minor resides. See section 182 of WESA.

In addition to serving the minor's parent(s) or guardian(s), the personal representative also must serve the Notice upon the Public Guardian and Trustee of British Columbia, <u>unless:</u>

- The minor is not a spouse or a child of the deceased,

- The will creates a trust for the interest of the minor and appoints a trustee for that trust, or

- The intended applicant is an executor or alternate executor of the deceased's estate.

Mentally incompetent persons

Delivery must be made to the Committee (does not include an attorney appointed under a Power of Attorney or a representative under a Representation Agreement) of the mentally incompetent person, as well as to the Public Guardian and Trustee of British Columbia. If there is no Committee, then the Notice is sent to the mentally incompetent person and the Public Guardian and Trustee of British Columbia.

If you are unsure if a person is mentally incompetent, all notices should be given out of an abundance of caution.

Missing persons

See explanation of missing intestate successors in Chapter 9.

Deceased beneficiaries

If the beneficiary predeceased the will-maker, WESA provisions apply regarding alternate beneficiaries, and notice then goes to those persons. See section 46(1) of WESA.

If the beneficiary died after the will-maker, notice should be given to the personal representative of the deceased beneficiary, as the gift will pass to the deceased beneficiary's estate.

If notice is required to be sent to the Public Guardian and Trustee, you must include, in addition to the standard P1 Notice, a further notice in writing that sets out the additional information required under Rule 25-1(13):

(13)   At the time that a notice is delivered to the Public Guardian and Trustee under subrule (8) or (11), the intended applicant must also deliver to the Public Guardian and Trustee a notice, in writing, setting out

(a)   The name of every other person to whom notice is required to be delivered under subrule (8) or (11), and

(b)   The most recent of each of the following that is known to the intended applicant about each of those persons:

(i)   The person's residential address, inside or outside British Columbia;
(ii)   The person's postal address, inside or outside British Columbia;
(iii)   The person's e-mail address, and;
(iv)   The person's fax number.

Note that if delivery of the P1 Notice and a copy of the will is required on the Public Guardian and Trustee, the Public Guardian and Trustee must be given the opportunity to respond, and the applicant must submit the written comments of the Public Guardian and Trustee to the court along with the application for the estate grant. The Public Guardian and Trustee must also be provided with copies of the filed application documents promptly after filing them. When you issue the filed documents to the Public Guardian and Trustee, you will also need to include a certified cheque or a bank draft in the amount of $336 (as of the date of this printing) made payable to the Public Guardian and Trustee of British Columbia, as they require payment for reviewing the application on behalf of a minor or mentally incompetent beneficiary.

In any estate where notice to the Public Guardian and Trustee is required, ensure that notice is properly prepared and delivered and that all relevant information is included. Failure to properly deliver notice in the form required could necessitate the notice having to be resent, and the 21-day waiting period restarted.

A sample P1 Notice is included at the end of this chapter.

Form P2 Submission for Estate Grant

The Submission for Estate Grant will be the document that initiates the probate proceeding. It sets out certain information about the deceased and the applicant, and the nature of the grant that is being sought.

The top part of the form is called the "style of cause" and it shows only the full legal name of the deceased (no known aliases included). Any aliases will be listed in Part 1 of the Submission for Estate Grant where indicated.

At the top right-hand corner of every document, the style of cause states the court file number and the location of the court registry. At this point in time, since no documents have been filed with the court registry, there is no court number to include. When you file the documents in court, the registry will stamp your documents with the file number that is assigned to your matter. The style of cause must be consistent on every document that you prepare that will be filed in the application process.

The "applicant" to be named on the first line of page one of the Submission for Estate Grant should be the personal representative. The P2 was designed using a check-box format to address the fact that a large number of applicants commencing probate applications do not have legal counsel and are therefore self-represented. Each numbered paragraph of the Submission for Estate Grant has multiple options. Those that are not selected should be deleted from the form; however, your submission will not be rejected by the court registry if you do *not* delete the sections that you are not including. Words within the standard paragraph being selected should not be deleted or changed if at all possible.

There are two different types of applications that you could be making with the P2 Submission for Estate Grant. The first one is a grant of probate. For this to be granted, you must have enough information to swear the Affidavit of Assets and Liabilities in Form P10. This means that you have contacted all of the financial institutions and they have provided the balances as of the date of death for the deceased, and that you have already been advised of all of the deceased's known assets and liabilities to the extent that the personal representative can swear is a complete listing. If you are missing even one account balance, you will not be able to obtain the grant of probate.

The second type of application you can make with the P2 Submission for Estate Grant is what is called an Authorization to Obtain Estate Information, in Form P18. This is required if you do not have enough information to swear the Affidavit of Assets and Liabilities. See the section Form P10 Affidavit of Assets and Liabilities later in this chapter for more information on Form P18.

On the first page of the P2 Submission, you have the option to ask the court to provide you with any number of court-certified copies of the estate grant or the Statement of Assets, Liabilities and Distribution. As a general practice, you should get one court-certified copy for each financial institution or organization where the deceased held assets (such as the Land Title Office or ICBC). That way, when you go to transfer the assets into your name as personal representative, you can provide each institution with a court-certified document for their records. For Land Title purposes, you will need a court-certified copy of the estate grant in addition to the court-certified copy of the Statement of Assets, Liabilities and Distribution.

The probate registry will keep the original estate grant and only provides the personal representative with a copy or court-certified copy. Therefore, if you need to certify or notarize a copy at a later date, a lawyer or a notary cannot certify that they have seen the original, but only a copy. This is why it is best practice to obtain a number of court-certified copies from the court registry, though they will charge you extra fees to do so.

Note that when completing the appropriate Schedule to the Submission for Estate Grant, the term "n/a" will not be accepted by the registry. If there is no person who meets the criteria of a particular category, simply write "none".

If there are other documents being filed with the application, such as a Notice of Renunciation in form P17, these documents should be listed in paragraph 7 of the Submission for Estate Grant.

A sample P2 Submission for Estate Grant is included at the end of this chapter.

Form P3 or P4 – Affidavit of Applicant

There are two options when completing the Affidavit of Applicant in a standard estate grant application. There is a short Form P3 and a long Form P4. As these are affidavits, they need to be "sworn" in front of a lawyer, notary, or a commissioner for taking oath and affidavits for British Columbia.

The Form P3 is the "standard" short-form affidavit where all the conditions listed in Rule 25-3(6) are met. It should be used if there are no abnormalities in the application.

A sample Form P3 is included at the end of this chapter.

The Form P4 is an expanded version of the Form P3 form and is intended to be used if there are any issues surrounding the will or its execution which require addressing. It should be used if any of the following apply:

- One or more testamentary documents dated later than the will have been found;

- There are issues regarding the will or its execution, for example:

  - o There are issues regarding formalities of execution;

  - o There are special circumstances surrounding the execution (ex. where the will-maker is blind or illiterate);

  - o There are interlineations, erasures, obliterations, or other alterations to the will;

  - o There are issues with the appearance of the will (ex. missing pages, attempted revocation, etc.).

- The will refers to one or more documents attached or not attached to the will (ex. memorandum, letter of wishes, etc.)

- There is a foreign applicant applying under section 139 of WESA.

A sample Form P4 is included at the end of this chapter.

In the case of multiple applicants, there are three ways to proceed:

1. One applicant can sign the P3 or P4, and the other(s) can sign the Form P8 (Affidavit in Support) – preferred method;

2. Both applicants can sign the same P3 or P4 form; or

3. Each applicant can sign a separate P3 or P4 form.

A sample Form P8 is included at the end of this chapter.

Form P9 Affidavit of Delivery

An Affidavit of Delivery in Form P9 is required to be sworn and submitted with the estate administration application. This form confirms with the court registry that the appropriate notices and copies of the will have been forwarded and delivered to the appropriate persons (see earlier in this chapter for more on Form P1 Notices). The Form P1 Notice that was issued to all these people needs to be attached to the end of the Affidavit of Delivery to demonstrate what was sent out.

If the personal representative is the person who actually put the P1 Notice and copy of the will in the mail box to send out, then the personal representative should be the one to swear the Affidavit of Delivery. If someone else mailed these documents on behalf of the personal representative, then this person should be the one to swear the Affidavit of Delivery.

In the body of the Affidavit of Delivery, you will list the name, address, and relationship to the deceased for each recipient of the Notice. Ensure that you include the date that you mailed the Notice to each person so that the registry can verify that you have waited the requisite 21 days before submitting the application.

A sample Form P9 Affidavit of Delivery is included at the end of this chapter.

Form P10 Affidavit of Assets and Liabilities

The Affidavit of Assets and Liabilities is designed to set out to the court all of the assets and liabilities of the estate. The affidavit has an exhibit attached to it called the "Statement of Assets, Liabilities, and Distribution" (SALD). The SALD is a form based on regulations passed under the *Probate Fee Act,* (SBC 1999, c 4.); however, it is important to note that the "Distribution" heading under the title is no longer a requirement. WESA changed the requirements so that only the assets and liabilities of the estate are required to be listed. You will need to set out all property of the deceased, irrespective of their nature, location, or value, that passes to the personal representative for distribution among the beneficiaries.

The P10 is the form that is used when the deceased was ordinarily resident in British Columbia. If the deceased was not ordinarily resident in British Columbia and all the property outside of British Columbia has or will be administered by a foreign personal representative, Form P11 would be used instead of the P10.

This affidavit is used by the court to determine how much in probate fees is payable by the estate.

The affidavit confirms that you are the applicant for the estate grant and that you have done a complete and diligent search for all property and debts of the deceased. It further confirms that, if you happen to come across any other property of the deceased that was not included in your sworn statement, you will immediately fill out a Supplemental Affidavit of Assets and Liabilities and file it with the court registry so that the court can reassess the amount of probate fees payable. Finally, it confirms that you will pay the probate fees as assessed by the probate registry.

The Form P10 and its exhibit requires the disclosure of the following:

- All property of the deceased that passes to the personal representative;

- The location of that property;

- The value of that property; and

- Any liabilities that encumber that property.

Note again that if there is property that is held in joint tenancy with a right of survivorship, the surviving joint tenant receives that property outright and that property does not need to be disclosed on the Form P10 and SALD unless it is being held in a bare trust on behalf of someone else, but that is beyond the scope of these materials.

Also, as previously mentioned, if there is a registered account such as an RRSP, RRIF, or a life insurance policy that names a specific designated beneficiary, that property does not pass to the estate, it passes directly to the specified beneficiary and therefore is not included in the SALD.

You are not allowed to put any unknowns in the SALD. Under the old rules, you could put "to be determined" for a value that you could not obtain readily; however, with the change in law, the court registry will no longer allow this except in very rare circumstances, such as if there was a pending class action law suit settlement that had yet to be distributed where it is impossible to know how much money the deceased will eventually receive. Furthermore, you are not allowed to use the term "n/a" and instead must use the term "None" or "Nil" if you do not possess those types of property.

If you are unable to obtain all the requisite information to fill out the P10 in its entirety, then you may need to first ask the court registry to issue you an Authorization to Obtain Estate Information, in Form P18, before obtaining the estate grant. This authorization is issued when you have submitted all other probate application materials to the court with the exception of the P10 Affidavit and exhibit. The probate registry will provide you with the filed Authorization which you can then send to any financial institution or organization that has not provided you with the information that you need to obtain the date of death balances for all assets and liabilities of the deceased. The institution then is required to provide you with this information within 30 days of receiving the Authorization.

Once you have received the information, you can fill in the Affidavit and SALD, swear that affidavit and submit it to the court where it joins the rest of the estate grant application materials, and then a grant can be issued if everything is in order.

As mentioned above, in the instance that the personal representative discovers an asset or liability that they were not aware of when they filed the P10 and the SALD, they will need to submit a Supplemental Affidavit in form P14 to disclose to the court the other assets or liabilities that should have been included in the P10.

Statement of Assets, Liabilities and Distribution (SALD)

Part I: Real Property

Real property refers to land, and includes any mortgages or registered encumbrances. If there is no real property owned by the deceased, then indicate "none" in this section, but do not leave it blank.

When you do your information gathering to determine the assets of the estate, you should perform a title search of the Land Title Office registry (you can go to the actual registry, or you may order the title search online using an online account, for a fee). This document will provide you with the particulars of the information needed for the SALD. The title search will list the owners and their full legal names (make sure you have this name in your Wills Notice Search and listed in your aliases in the P2 Submission document). It will tell you how the property is owned: whether the deceased was the sole owner, whether they owned the property as joint tenants (if the surviving joint tenant is alive, the real property will not be listed on the SALD), or whether they owned the property as tenants in common (they may be tenants as to an undivided half interest, or as other percentage interests, and this needs to be expressed on the SALD. You will only state the value of the deceased's interest in the property). If there is more than one owner on the title search, if the title search does not expressly state "as joint tenants", and if it is silent on how much of an interest is owned by each owner, the default presumption is that the title is held as tenants in common in equal shares.

You will need the Parcel Identifier Number or "PID", which is a 9-digit number, as well as the "legal description" of the interest in property, and the civic address of the property. You will also need to have the BC Property Assessment value for the current year so that you can state on the SALD how much the property is worth. Alternatively, you can obtain an appraisal from a property appraiser or obtain the market value from a real estate agent. Be careful if you are just listing the BC Property Assessment value, as it might be significantly different from the market value depending on various factors. Note that if you only disclose the assessed value and then end up selling the property for a lot more than what was stated on the SALD, you might open up the estate to a capital gains charge, taxable at the deceased's marginal tax rate.

Once you have stated the value of the property, you can then deduct any registered mortgage listed on title from the gross value of the property. You need to ensure that you have the exact mortgage owing as of the date of death. You cannot use a standard bank statement for this purpose and must contact the financial institution to find out exactly what the balance was from the date of death.

Part II: Personal Property

All of the other assets of the deceased, <u>as of the date of death</u>, must be listed in this section. This includes tangible (collections, art, vehicles, etc.) and intangible (bank accounts, investments, stocks and bonds or other securities, etc.) property.

Tangible property will include household possessions, but these generally have no real commercial value. Of course, there are exceptions but if nothing is particularly valuable, you can state that household possessions have a "nil" value as of the date of death or a "nominal" value, which is counted as zero balance towards the gross value of the estate. Furniture can be given a value estimate based on what it might be worth at a garage sale. If the furniture was held jointly and passed to the surviving joint tenant, you can list that in the statement as well.

In any event, you may want to retain the services of a qualified appraiser if there are unique valuables or any possessions whose value you are unsure of.

Ensure that you have done a complete and diligent search of the papers and files of the deceased to make completely sure that you include everything that the deceased owned as of the date of death. Note that for accounts and intangible property you cannot use monthly statements to provide the balance, but must acquire the exact value as of the date of death and be sure to include any accrued interest to the date of death if an account is interest-bearing.

Any death benefits or issuances from Old Age Security or the Canada Pension Plan for the month of death should be included in the statement. Veteran's benefits are included but be cautioned that survivor's benefits are not included.

If the deceased owned an insurance policy or a pension that did not list a designated beneficiary, the proceeds will fall to the estate. You will need to include all information known about the policy or pension in the Statement.

There is no longer any need to list a safety deposit box in the personal property section; however, if there are contents of value in the safety deposit box, those need to be included.

Note that intangible assets, such as bank accounts and investments, are generally deemed to be 'within' British Columbia even if the branch location is outside of British Columbia and therefore are subject to probate fees.

Part III: Liabilities

All debts or accounts payable as of the date of death need to be listed in this section. You need to include whether the debt has been paid or if it remains unpaid. Before any assets of the estate are distributed to any beneficiary or intestate successor, all of the debts listed need to be paid.

You can notify the creditors of the death of the deceased and ensure that you obtain the outstanding balance as of the date of death from them. You can advise creditors that they will need to wait to be paid until you receive the estate grant and have access to the accounts. Some creditors will halt the interest accruing from the date of death, some will not.

The accounts of the deceased will usually be frozen until such time as an estate grant is received. However, the bank will usually issue a cheque for the funeral expenses and will issue a bank draft for probate fees, but you need to produce the amount owing on each for them to issue the correct amount.

The probate registry only requires you to list liabilities that charge or encumber a specific item of property (like a mortgage), or if there is a creditor that has a claim that is over $10,000 (as they essentially become a beneficiary of the estate).

A sample Form P10 and SALD are included at the end of this chapter.

Application for Grant of Administration with Will Annexed

This type of estate grant is obtained when there is a will of the deceased, but there is no executor named, or the executor and/or alternate executor is otherwise unable or unwilling to act. The named executor may have predeceased the will-maker or may not have the mental capability to prepare and administer the estate. In this scenario, the will is still valid and will be submitted to probate, but an administrator needs to step up to be granted administrator of the estate. If the named executor is still alive, the proposed administrator needs to obtain a Renunciation (see section in Chapter 3 on Renunciations) from the named executor. The same order for priority for administrators applies as an intestate estate, under section 130 of WESA. See the following chapter with respect to intestate estates. As with an intestate estate, if there are people who outrank you in priority to be the administrator, you should obtain signed consents from those people and retain them on your file. They do not need to be filed in the court registry but may need to be relied upon later on.

The application documents to submit for a Grant of Administration with Will Annexed are the same application documents for a Grant of Administration where there is a will, as earlier in this chapter. The only difference will be that you may have to select different boxes to ensure that you are stating that you are applying not as the executor, but for the administration with will annexed. Be sure if the named executor is alive and you have received a Notice of Renunciation in form P17 to include it in your estate grant application package to the court registry.

PRE-GRANT ESTATE ADMINISTRATION CHECKLIST

		N/A	Requested	Received
1.	Completed Estate Questionnaire			
2.	Land Title Office search(es)			
3.	Wills Notice Search (wait until all LTO searches obtained)			
4.	Death Certificate			
5.	Letters requesting information re: assets mailed out			
6.	Information regarding beneficiaries/next-of-kin/ intestate successors received			
			Done	Date
7.	Notices of Proposed Application in Relation to Estate mailed: by client ☐ by solicitor ☐			
8.	Notice to Public Guardian and Trustee			
9.	Application documents prepared			

10.	Application documents executed			
11.	Application filed with probate registry			
12.	Application approved and probate fees confirmed			
13.	Probate fees requested			
14.	Probate fee received and paid to probate registry			
15.	Grant received			

Form P1 (Rule 25-2(3))

NOTICE OF PROPOSED APPLICATION IN RELATION TO ESTATE

TAKE NOTICE THAT:

The applicant, *[name of applicant]*, proposes to apply, in the Vancouver court registry, for a grant of probate in relation to the estate of the deceased described below who died on *[dd/mmm/yyyy]*.

Full legal name of deceased: *[full legal name]*

Last residential address of the deceased: *[Include street number or post office box, city/town, province, country and postal code.]*

[X]   This application relates to the will of the deceased dated *[dd/mmm/yyyy]*, a copy of which will is provided with this notice.

AND TAKE NOTICE THAT:

(1)   Before obtaining the foregoing grant or resealing, the applicant may be granted an authorization to obtain estate information or an authorization to obtain resealing information, as the case may be, in relation to that grant or resealing for the purposes of obtaining financial information in relation to the grant or resealing.

(2)   You have a right to oppose, by filing a notice of dispute in accordance with Rule 25-10(1),

(a)   if the intended application is for an estate grant, the granting of either or both of an authorization to obtain estate information and the estate grant, or

(b)   if the intended application is for a resealing, the granting of either or both of an authorization to obtain resealing information and the resealing.

(3)   You may or may not be entitled to claim against the estate for relief, including a claim under

(a)   the *Family Law Act*, or

(b)   Division 6 of Part 4 of the *Wills, Estates and Succession Act.*

(4)   If you choose to take a step referred to in paragraph (2) or (3), you must do so within the time limited by any relevant rule of court or other enactment.

(5) You may consult with your own lawyer concerning your interest in, or rights against, the estate.

(6) After the applicant has filed a submission for estate grant or submission for resealing, you may apply for an order requiring the applicant to provide security unless the applicant is the Public Guardian and Trustee. Filing a notice of dispute will prevent a grant from being issued before you are able to apply for the order requiring security.

(7) An authorization to obtain estate information, an authorization to obtain resealing information or a grant may issue to the applicant, or a foreign grant may be resealed, on any date that is *at least 21 days* after the date on which this notice is delivered to you or on any earlier date ordered by the court.

(8) If an authorization to obtain estate information issues to the applicant, the applicant may apply for a grant without further notice. If an authorization to obtain resealing information issues to the applicant, the applicant may apply for the resealing of the foreign grant without further notice to you.

(9) If a grant issues to the applicant, the applicant must provide, if there is a will, to the beneficiaries or, if there is no will, to intestate successors of the deceased, an accounting as to how the estate was administered and how the estate assets were distributed, and if a foreign grant is resealed as a result of the application, the intended applicant must provide, if there is a will, to the beneficiaries or, if there is no will, to intestate successors of the deceased, an accounting as to how the estate comprising the assets to which the resealed grant applies was administered and how those assets were distributed.

INFORMATION ABOUT EACH APPLICANT

Name: *[name]*

Mailing address: *[Include street number or post office box, city/town, province, country and postal code.]*

    [X] This applicant is an individual and ordinarily lives

    [X] at the mailing address noted above

ADDRESS FOR SERVICE OF APPLICANT

    [X] The applicant's address for service is

Street address for service:

Fax number address for service (if any):

E-mail address for service (if any):

Telephone number:

Date: [dd/mmm/yyyy].

_____
Signature of [type name]
[ ]   lawyer for applicant
[ ]   applicant

Nicole Garton, LLB, TEP

Form P2 (Rule 25-3(2))

No.
Vancouver Registry

In the Supreme Court of British Columbia

In the Matter of the Estate of *[legal name of deceased]*, deceased

SUBMISSION FOR ESTATE GRANT

This submission for estate grant is submitted on behalf of: *[name(s) of applicant(s)]*.

I, *[name of applicant]*, am applying for the following in relation to the estate of the deceased described in Part 1 of this submission for estate grant (the "deceased"):

[X]   Grant of probate

[Check whichever one of the immediately following 2 boxes is correct.]

[X]   I am/We are submitting with this submission for estate grant an affidavit of assets and liabilities in Form P10 or P11 and therefore do not require an authorization to obtain estate information.

[ ]   I am/We are seeking an authorization to obtain estate information so that I/ we can secure the information necessary to prepare and submit an affidavit of assets and liabilities for estate grant.

[X]   I request *[number of copies]* court-certified copies of the estate grant. *and 1 court-certified copy of the Statement of Assets, Liabilities & Distribution.

[ ]   I request *[number of copies]* court-certified copies of the authorization to obtain estate information.

This submission for estate grant has 4 Parts:

Part 1: Information about the Deceased

Part 2: Contact Information for the Applicant(s)

Part 3: Documents Filed with this submission for estate grant

Part 4: Schedule

Date: *[dd/mm/yyyy]*

_____

Signature of [lawyer]

[x]   lawyer for applicant(s)

Part 1: INFORMATION ABOUT THE DECEASED

Full legal name of deceased: *[first name], [middle name(s)], [last name/family name]*

Other names in which the deceased held or may have held an interest in property:

1

2

3

Last residential address of the deceased:

        Street number and street name: *[specify]*
        OR Post office box: *[specify]*
        City/Town: *[specify]*
        Province: *[specify]*
        Country: *[specify]*
        Postal Code: *[specify]*

Deceased's date of death: *[month, day, year]*

[Check whichever one of the immediately following 3 boxes is correct and provide any required information.]

    [X]   The deceased was neither a Nisga'a citizen nor a member of a treaty first nation.

    [X]   The deceased was a Nisga'a citizen.

    [X]   The deceased was a member of the [name] treaty first nation.

Part 2: CONTACT INFORMATION FOR THE APPLICANT(S)

Street address for service:

Fax number address for service (if any):

E-mail address for service (if any):

Telephone number:

Part 3: DOCUMENTS FILED WITH THIS SUBMISSION FOR ESTATE GRANT

1 *[Check whichever one of the immediately following 2 boxes is correct and file the specified affidavit(s).]*

   [X] There is one applicant to this submission for estate grant and

   (a) the applicant has made an affidavit in Form *[Select whichever one of the following 5 choices is correct—P3/P4/P5/P6/P7]*, and

   (b) that affidavit is filed with this submission for estate grant.

   [ ] There are 2 or more applicants to this submission for estate grant and

   (a) at least one of the applicants has made an affidavit in Form *[Select whichever one of the following 5 choices is correct—P3/P4/P5/ P6/P7]*,

   (b) that affidavit is filed with this submission for estate grant, and

   (c) the remaining applicant(s) has/have made (an) affidavit(s) in Form P8 and that/those affidavit(s) is/are filed with this submission for estate grant.

2 [X] Filed with this submission for estate grant is the following Affidavit of Delivery in Form P9 that confirms that the documents referred to in Rule 25-2 were delivered to all of the persons to whom, under that rule, the documents were required to be delivered:

   Affidavit of *[name]* sworn *[month, day, year]*

   [ ] No affidavit of delivery is attached. In accordance with Rule 25-2, no one, other than the applicant(s), is entitled to notice.

3   Filed with this submission for estate grant are 2 copies of the certificate of the chief executive officer under the Vital Statistics Act indicating the results of a search for a wills notice filed by or on behalf of the deceased.

4   [X]   This application is for a grant of probate, or a grant of administration with will annexed, in relation to the will of the deceased dated *[month, day, year]*, and filed with this submission for estate grant is the originally signed version of the will.

5   [X]   This application is for a grant of probate or a grant of administration with will annexed and there are no orders affecting the validity or content of the will referred to in section 4.

5   [X]   This application is for a grant of probate or a grant of administration with will annexed and the following order(s) affect(s) the validity or content of the will referred to in section 4:

[If you checked the immediately preceding box, describe any applicable orders, indicate if they have been filed in this proceeding and file any described orders that have not yet been filed in this proceeding.]

      1   Order dated *[month, day, year]*

          [ ]   This order has been filed in this proceeding.

          [ ]   This order has not yet been filed in this proceeding and I am/we are therefore filing a copy of the order with this submission for estate grant.

      2   Order dated *[month, day, year]*

          [ ]   This order has been filed in this proceeding.

          [ ]   This order has not yet been filed in this proceeding and I am/we are therefore filing a copy of the order with this submission for estate grant.

      3   etc.

6   [X]   This application is for a grant of probate, a grant of administration with will annexed, an ancillary grant of probate or an ancillary grant of administration with will annexed and the will referred to in section 4 does not refer to any documents or refers only to documents attached to the will.

6   [ ]   This application is for a grant of probate, a grant of administration with will annexed, an ancillary grant of probate or an ancillary grant of administration with will annexed and filed with this submission for estate grant is/are the following document(s), which document(s) is/are all of the documents referred to in, but not attached to, the will referred to in section 4:

1

2

3

7   [X]   No documents other than those described elsewhere in this submission for estate grant are filed with this submission for estate grant.

7   [X]   In addition to the documents described elsewhere in this submission for estate grant, the following documents are filed with this submission for estate grant:

1

2

3

8   [X]   All documents filed with this submission for estate grant are written in the English language.

Part 4: SCHEDULE

1   [X]   Attached to this submission for estate grant is a Schedule for Grant of Probate or Grant of Administration with Will Annexed.

The Heritage Trust Estate Administration Boot Camp

SCHEDULE FOR GRANT OF PROBATE OR
GRANT OF ADMINISTRATION WITH WILL ANNEXED

1   Criteria

    (a)   he or she is named in the will as executor or alternate executor;

    (b)   he or she is a co-executor with the applicant(s) (i.e. has a right to make an application for an estate grant that is equal to the applicant's(s') right to make that application);

    (c)   he or she has not renounced executorship;

    (d)   he or she is alive at the date of this submission for estate grant;

    (e)   he or she has not become incapable of managing his or her affairs.

        [X]   There is no person who meets all of the foregoing criteria.

        [X]   The following person(s) meet(s) all of the foregoing criteria:

           1

           2

           3   etc.

2   Listed in each of the following paragraphs is every person who falls within the class of persons identified by that paragraph:

[Provide under each of the following paragraphs the full name of each person to whom the paragraph applies, whether or not that person is named elsewhere in this submission for estate grant.] [List each named person on a separate line. Do not leave any paragraph blank or indicate "Not applicable"; clearly state why a paragraph does not apply.]

    (a)   spouse, if any, of the deceased: *[see section 2 of the Wills, Estates and Succession Act]: [Provide the appropriate response(s), as applicable: spouse [provide name of spouse]/no currently living spouse as defined by section 2 of the Wills, Estates and Succession Act [provide name of spouse and indicate "(deceased)"]/other former spouse(s) [provide name(s) of other former spouse(s) and indicate "(former spouse)"]/never married.]: [specify]*

(b) child(ren), if any, of the deceased: *[Provide the appropriate response(s), as applicable: living child(ren) of deceased [provide name(s) of child(ren)]/any child(ren) of the deceased who died before the deceased [provide name(s) of child(ren) and indicate "(deceased)"]/no children.]: [specify]*

(c) each person, if any, who is a beneficiary under the will and is not named in paragraph (a) or (b): *[List each living beneficiary and all beneficiaries who have died before the deceased in this application and indicate "(living)" or "(deceased)", as applicable.]: [specify]*

(d) each person, if any, who would have been an intestate successor if the deceased had not left a will and who is not named in paragraph (a), (b) or (c) *[List all living persons who would be entitled to inherit on intestacy and their relationship to the deceased.]: [specify]*

(e) each citor, if any, not named in paragraph (a), (b), (c) or (d): *[specify]*

The Heritage Trust Estate Administration Boot Camp

Form P3 (Rule 25-3(2))

This is the 1st affidavit of
[name] in this case and was
made on _____/August/2019.

No.
Vancouver Registry

In the Supreme Court of British Columbia

In the Matter of the Estate of *[legal name of deceased]*, deceased

AFFIDAVIT OF APPLICANT FOR GRANT OF PROBATE OR GRANT OF ADMINISTRATION WITH WILL ANNEXED

I, *[name]*, of *[address]*, *[occupation]*, SWEAR (OR AFFIRM) THAT:

1   I am the applicant referred to in the submission for estate grant in relation to the estate of *[legal name of deceased]* (the "deceased") and in relation to the document that is identified in section 4 of Part 3 of the submission for estate grant as the will (the "will"), and am applying for

        [X]   a grant of probate.

2   [X]   I am an individual and ordinarily live at the following location:

City/town: *[specify]*

Province/state: *[specify]*

Country: *[specify]*

3   All of paragraphs (a) to (k) of Rule 25-3(6) are true and I am therefore authorized under Rule 25-3(6) to swear this affidavit.

4   [X]   I am named as an executor or alternate executor as *[name as it appears in the will]* in the will and my appointment has not been revoked under section 56(2) of the Wills, Estates and Succession Act or by a codicil to the will.

                [Check whichever of the following 2 boxes is correct]

        [ ]   No other persons are named in the will as executor.

        [ ]   Other persons are named in the will as executor and, of those, the following person(s) is/are not named as an applicant on the

submission for estate grant for the reason shown after his/her/their name(s):

[Complete tne following for each named person.]

> *[name]* is not named as an applicant on the submission for estate grant because he/she [ ] has renounced executorship [ ] is deceased [ ] other *[briefly set out reason]*

5   [X]   I am not obliged under Rule 25-3(11) to deliver a filed copy of this submission for estate grant to the Public Guardian and Trustee.

6   I am satisfied that a diligent search for a testamentary document of the deceased has been made in each place that could reasonably be considered to be a place where a testamentary document may be found, including, without limitation, in all places where the deceased usually kept his or her documents and that no testamentary document that is dated later than the date of the will has been found.

7   I believe that the will is the last will of the deceased that deals with property in British Columbia.

8   I am not aware of any grant of probate or administration, or equivalent, having been issued, in relation to the deceased, in British Columbia or in any other jurisdiction.

9   I believe that the will complies with the requirements of Division 1 of Part 4 of the Wills, Estates and Succession Act and I am not aware of any issues that would call into question the validity or contents of the will.

10   I have read the submission for estate grant and the other documents referred to in that document and I believe that the information contained in that submission for estate grant and those documents is correct and complete.

11   I will administer according to law all of the deceased's estate, I will prepare an accounting as to how the estate was administered and I acknowledge that, in doing this, I will be subject to the legal responsibility of a personal representative.

SWORN (OR AFFIRMED)	)
BEFORE ME at *[location]*,	)
British Columbia,	)
on *[day month, year]* .	)
	)
_____	) _____
A commissioner for taking affidavits	) DEPONENT'S NAME
for British Columbia	)

The Heritage Trust Estate Administration Boot Camp

Form P4 (Rule 25-3(2))

This is the 1st affidavit of *[name]* in this case and was made on _____.

No.
Vancouver Registry

In the Supreme Court of British Columbia

In the Matter of the Estate of *[legal name of deceased]*, deceased

AFFIDAVIT OF APPLICANT FOR GRANT OF PROBATE OR GRANT OF ADMINISTRATION WITH WILL ANNEXED

I, *[name]*, of *[address]*, *[occupation]*, SWEAR (OR AFFIRM) THAT:

1. I am the applicant/one of the applicants referred to in the submission for estate grant in relation to the estate of *[legal name of deceased]* (the "deceased") and in relation to the document that is identified in section 4 of Part 3 of the submission for estate grant as the will (the "will"), and am applying for:

    [Check whichever one of the immediately following 2 boxes is correct.]

    [ ] a grant of probate.

    [ ] a grant of administration with will annexed.

2. *[Check whichever one of the immediately following 2 boxes is correct and provide any required information.]*

    [ ] The applicant on whose behalf this affidavit is sworn is not an individual and I am authorized by the applicant to swear this affidavit on the applicant's behalf.

    [ ] I am an individual and ordinarily live at the following location:

    City/town: *[specify]*

    Province/state: *[specify]*

    Country: *[specify]*

[Check the box for whichever one of the immediately following section 3's is correct and provide any required information.]

3.   [ ]   I am named as an executor or alternate executor as *[name as it appears in the will]* in the will and my appointment has not been revoked under section 56(2) of the *Wills, Estates and Succession Act* or by a codicil to the will.

[If you checked the immediately preceding box, check whichever one of the immediately following 2 boxes is correct and complete any required information.]

[ ]   No other persons are named in the will as executor.

[ ]   Other persons are named in the will as executor and, of those, the following person(s) is/are not named as an applicant on the submission for estate grant for the reason shown after his/her/their name(s):

[Complete the following for each named person.]

[name] is not named as an applicant on the submission for estate grant because he/she [] has renounced executorship [] is deceased [] other *[briefly set out reason]*

3.   [ ]   I am not named as an executor or alternate executor in the will, and am a person referred to in paragraph *[specify]* of section 131 of the *Wills, Estates and Succession Act.*

3.   [ ]   I am an attorney of a foreign personal representative and am making application under section 139 of the *Wills, Estates and Succession Act.*

4.   *[Check whichever one of the immediately following 2 boxes is correct.]*

[ ]   I am not obliged under Rule 25-3(11) to deliver a filed copy of this submission for estate grant to the Public Guardian and Trustee.

[ ]   I am obliged under Rule 25-3(11) to deliver a filed copy of this submission for estate grant to the Public Guardian and Trustee.

5.   I am satisfied that a diligent search for a testamentary document of the deceased has been made in each place that could reasonably be considered to be a place where a testamentary document may be found, including, without limitation, in all places where the deceased usually kept his or her documents and

[Check whichever one of the immediately following 2 boxes is correct and provide any required information.]

[ ]   no testamentary document of the deceased dated later than the will has been found

[ ]   one or more testamentary documents dated later than the will have been found. I believe that the later testamentary document(s) is/are invalid or otherwise not relevant to this application for the following reasons: *[briefly state the reasons]*.

6.   *[Check whichever one of the immediately following 2 boxes is correct.]*

[ ]   I am not aware of there being any issues respecting execution of the will. *[Go to section 7]*

[ ]   I believe that the following issue(s) respecting execution apply(ies) to the will and I am not aware of there being any other issues respecting execution of the will:

[If you checked the second of the immediately preceding 2 boxes, complete each of the following paragraphs (a) to (d) as required.]

    (a)   <u>Attestation Clause</u>

    <u>[the portion of the will that identifies the persons who signed the will as witnesses to the will-maker's signature]</u>

    [Check whichever one of the immediately following 2 boxes is correct.]

    [ ]   None of this paragraph (a) applies to the will.

    [ ]   The will does not contain an attestation clause or contains an attestation clause that is not sufficient to show that the requirements of Division 1 of Part 4 of the *Wills, Estates and Succession Act* were met when the will was signed.

    [If you checked the second of the immediately preceding 2 boxes, check whichever one of the immediately following 5 boxes is correct and provide any required information.]

[ ] pursuant to Rule 25-3(15), submitted for filing with the submission for estate grant is an affidavit of *[name]* sworn *[month, day, year]* who was a subscribing witness.

[ ] an affidavit from a subscribing witness cannot be obtained, and pursuant to Rule 25-3(16)(a), submitted for filing with the submission for estate grant, is an affidavit of *[name]* sworn *[month, day, year]* who was a person present when the will was signed.

[ ] neither an affidavit from a subscribing witness nor an affidavit sworn by a person present when the will was signed can be obtained, and pursuant to Rule 25-3(16)(b), submitted for filing with the submission for estate grant is/are the following affidavit(s) confirming the signatures of the will-maker and subscribing witnesses:

    1.   the affidavit of *[name]* sworn *[month, day, year]*

    2.   the affidavit of *[name]* sworn *[month, day, year]*

[ ] none of an affidavit from a subscribing witness, an affidavit sworn by a person present when the will was signed and an affidavit confirming the signatures of the will-maker and subscribing witnesses can be obtained, and pursuant to Rule 25-3(16)(c), submitted for filing with the submission for estate grant, is an affidavit of *[name]* sworn *[month, day, year]* which affidavit sets out circumstances intended to raise a presumption in favour of the proper execution of the will.

[ ] the will is valid as to the formal requirements for making the will and is admissible to probate under section 80 of the *Wills, Estates and Succession Act*, and submitted for filing with the submission for estate grant is/are the following affidavit(s) confirming that validity:

    1.   the affidavit of *[name]* sworn *[month, day, year]*

    2.   the affidavit of *[name]* sworn *[month, day, year]*

(b)   <u>Military Will</u>

[Check whichever one of the immediately following 2 boxes is correct.]

The Heritage Trust Estate Administration Boot Camp

[ ]   This paragraph (b) does not apply to the will.

[ ]   I believe that the will was made by a person referred to in Rule 25-3(17) and is in a form permitted by section 38 of the *Wills, Estates and Succession Act*, and attached as Exhibit *[specify]* to this affidavit is *[describe nature of evidence attached]* as evidence that the will-maker was authorized to make a will in that form at the time the will was made and that the will was executed in accordance with the requirements of section 38 of the *Wills, Estates and Succession Act*.

(c)   <u>Special Circumstances</u>

[Check whichever one of the immediately following 2 boxes is correct.]

[ ]   None of this paragraph (c) applies to the will.

[ ]   I believe that at the time of the making of the will, the will-maker

[If you checked the second of the immediately preceding 2 boxes, check whichever one or more of the immediately following 5 boxes is correct.]

    [ ]   was blind

    [ ]   was illiterate

    [ ]   did not fully understand the language in which the will was written

    [ ]   signed by a means of a mark instead of handwritten words

    [ ]   directed another person to sign the will on behalf of the will-maker in the will-maker's presence

and

[If you checked one or more of the immediately preceding 5 boxes, check whichever one of the immediately following 3 boxes is correct and provide any required information.]

[ ] the attestation clause in the will indicates that the circumstance(s) referred to above applied to the will-maker at the time of the signing of the will.

[ ] the following affidavit(s) is/are submitted for filing with the submission for estate grant as evidence that the requirements of the *Wills, Estates and Succession Act* relating to the execution of the will were met and that the will-maker knew and approved of the content of the will:

1. the affidavit of *[name]* sworn *[month, day, year]*

2. the affidavit of *[name]* sworn *[month, day, year]*

[ ] the will is valid as to the formal requirements for making the will and is admissible to probate under section 80 of the *Wills, Estates and Succession Act*, and submitted for filing with the submission for estate grant is/are the following affidavit(s) confirming that validity:

1. the affidavit of *[name]* sworn *[month, day, year]*

2. the affidavit of *[name]* sworn *[month, day, year]*

(d)   <u>Other Issues</u>

[Check whichever one of the immediately following 2 boxes is correct.]

[ ] There are no other issues relating to proper execution of the will.

[ ] The following is/are the other issue(s) relating to proper execution of the will:

[set out the issue] and attached as Exhibit [specify] to this affidavit is [describe].

7.   *[Check whichever one of the immediately following 2 boxes is correct and provide any required information.]*

[ ] I am not aware of there being any interlineations, erasures or obliterations in, or other alterations to, the will. *[Go to section 8.]*

The Heritage Trust Estate Administration Boot Camp

[ ]   There are interlineations, erasures or obliterations in, or other alterations to, the will.

[If you checked the second of the immediately preceding 2 boxes, complete the immediately following paragraph (a) if there are one or more interlineations in the will, paragraph (b) if there are one or more erasures or obliterations in the will, and paragraph (c) if there are one or more alterations in the will.]

(a)   <u>Interlineations</u>

[ ]   There are one or more interlineations in the will, and the following applies to each of those interlineations:

[If you checked the immediately preceding box, check whichever one of the immediately following 4 boxes is correct and provide any required information.]

[ ]   I believe that the interlineation was made in accordance with the requirements of Division 1 of Part 4 of the *Wills, Estates and Succession Act* relating to the execution of a will.

[ ]   I believe that the interlineation was authenticated by the re-execution of the will or by the subsequent execution of a codicil.

[ ]   I cannot check either of the 2 immediately preceding boxes but believe that the interlineation should form part of the will as it was present when the will was signed, and, pursuant to Rule 253(20)(a), submitted for filing with the submission for estate grant is/are the following affidavit(s):

1.   the affidavit of *[name]* sworn *[month, day, year]*

2.   the affidavit of *[name]* sworn *[month, day, year]*

[ ]   I have no information to suggest that the interlineation reflects the will-maker's intentions.

[ ]   There are one or more interlineations in the will, and none of the foregoing boxes applies to all of those interlineations.

(b)   <u>Words Erased or Obliterated</u>

[ ]   Words in the will were erased or obliterated and

[If you checked the immediately preceding box, check whichever one of the immediately following 2 boxes is correct and provide any required information.]

[ ]   in each erasure or obliteration in the will, the words erased or obliterated are entirely effaced and cannot be ascertained on inspection.

[ ]   the will contains at least one erasure or obliteration in which the words erased or obliterated are not entirely effaced and can be read, and the following applies to each of the erasures or obliterations that are not entirely effaced and can be read:

[If you checked the second of the immediately preceding 2 boxes, check whichever one of the immediately following 4 boxes is correct and provide any required information.]

[ ]   I believe that the erasure or obliteration was made in accordance with the requirements of Division 1 of Part 4 of the *Wills, Estates and Succession Act* relating to the execution of a will.

[ ]   I believe that the erasure or obliteration was authenticated by the re-execution of the will or by the subsequent execution of a codicil.

[ ]   I believe that the words erased or obliterated should not form part of the will and, pursuant to Rule 25-3(21)(a), submitted for filing with the submission for estate grant is/are the following affidavit(s):

1.   the affidavit of *[name]* sworn *[month, day, year]*

2.   the affidavit of *[name]* sworn *[month, day, year]*

[ ]   I have no information to suggest that the interlineation reflects the will-maker's intentions.

The Heritage Trust Estate Administration Boot Camp

[ ]   There are one or more erasures or obliterations in the will in which the words erased or obliterated are not entirely effaced and can be read, and none of the foregoing boxes applies to all of those erasures or obliterations.

(c)   <u>Other Issues</u>

[ ]   I believe that the following issue(s) arise from the appearance of the will:

[If you checked the immediately preceding box, check whichever one or more of the immediately following 5 boxes are correct.]

[ ]   It appears that an attempt was made to revoke the will.

[ ]   It appears that a page or document was previously attached to the will but is missing.

[ ]   It appears that the will is incomplete.

[ ]   It appears that the will has been altered by an alteration that was not made by the will-maker in compliance with the *Wills, Estates and Succession Act.*

[ ]   It appears that *[specify]*

and submitted for filing in support of the submission for estate grant is/are the following affidavit(s):

1.   the affidavit of *[name]* sworn *[month, day, year]*

2.   the affidavit of *[name]* sworn *[month, day, year]*

8.   *[Check whichever one of the immediately following 2 boxes is correct.]*

[ ]   The will does not refer to any documents or refers only to documents attached to the will.

[ ]   The will refers to one or more documents not attached to the will and

[If you checked the second of the immediately preceding 2 boxes, complete the following for each document that is referred to in, but not attached to, the will.]

[ ] a copy of *[identify document],*

[Check whichever one of the immediately following 2 boxes is correct.]

[ ] is attached as Exhibit *[specify]* to this affidavit.

[ ] cannot be obtained by the applicant.

9. *[Check whichever one of the immediately following 2 boxes is correct.]*

[ ] I am not aware of any grant of probate or administration, or equivalent, having been issued, in relation to the deceased, in British Columbia or in any other jurisdiction.

[ ] The following grant(s) of probate or administration, or equivalent, has/ have been issued, in relation to the deceased, in British Columbia or in another jurisdiction: *[specify].* I believe that that grant is/those grants are not relevant to this application for the following reasons: *[briefly state the reasons].*

10. I have read the submission for estate grant and the other documents referred to in that document and I believe that the information contained in that submission for estate grant and those documents is correct and complete.

11. I will administer according to law all of the deceased's estate, I will prepare an accounting as to how the estate was administered and I acknowledge that, in doing this, I will be subject to the legal responsibility of a personal representative.

SWORN (OR AFFIRMED) BEFORE ME at *[location],* British Columbia, on *[month, day, year]*	)))))))
_____ A commissioner for taking affidavits for British Columbia	))))
[print name or affix stamp of commissioner]	

_____
DEPONENT'S NAME

The Heritage Trust Estate Administration Boot Camp

Form P8 (Rule 25-3(2))

This is the 1st affidavit
of *[name]* in this case and was
made on *[month, day, year]*

No.
Vancouver Registry

In the Supreme Court of British Columbia

In the Matter of the Estate of *[legal name of deceased]*, deceased

AFFIDAVIT IN SUPPORT OF APPLICATION FOR ESTATE GRANT

I, *[name]*, of *[address]*, *[occupation]*, SWEAR (OR AFFIRM) THAT:

1   I am one of the applicants referred to in the submission for estate grant in relation to the estate of *[legal name of deceased]* (the "deceased").

2   I have read the affidavit in Form *[set out whichever one of the following 5 choices is correct–P3/P4/P5/P6/P7]* sworn *[month, day, year]* by *[name of person who swore that affidavit]* and there is nothing in that affidavit that I know to be inaccurate.

3   I have read the submission for estate grant and the other documents referred to in that document and I believe that the information contained in that submission for estate grant and those documents is correct and complete.

4   I will administer according to law the deceased's estate to which the submission for estate grant relates and I acknowledge that, in doing this, I will be subject to the legal responsibility of a personal representative.

SWORN (OR AFFIRMED)	)
BEFORE ME at *[location]*,	)
British Columbia,	)
on *[month, day, year]*	)
	)
	)
_____	) _____
A commissioner for taking affidavits	) DEPONENT'S NAME
for British Columbia	)

Nicole Garton, LLB, TEP

Form P9 (Rule 25-3(2))

This is the 1st affidavit
of *[name]* in this case and was
made on *[month, day, year]*

No.
Vancouver Registry

In the Supreme Court of British Columbia

In the Matter of the Estate of *[legal name of deceased]*, deceased

AFFIDAVIT OF DELIVERY

I, *[name]*, of *[address]*, *[occupation]*, SWEAR (OR AFFIRM) THAT:

1   Attached to this affidavit and marked as Exhibit A is a copy of a notice of proposed application in Form P1 (the "notice").

2   I delivered a copy of the notice, along with a copy of the will, *[identify any other documents]* to the following persons as follows:

[ ]   by mailing it/them to the following persons by ordinary mail on *[date]*:

[name of person who received delivery by ordinary mail], a *[relationship]*,

[name of person who received delivery by ordinary mail], a *[relationship]*,

[ ]   by handing it/them to and leaving it/them with the following persons as follows on *[date]*:

[name of person who received personal delivery], a *[relationship]*,

[name of person who received personal delivery], a *[relationship]*,

[ ]   by sending it/them to the following persons by e-mail, fax or other electronic means to that person on *[date]*:

[name of person who received delivery by e-mail, fax or other electronic means], a *[relationship]*,

[name of person who received delivery by e-mail, fax or other electronic means], a *[relationship]*,

[If you checked the third of the immediately preceding 3 boxes, check both of the immediately following boxes. If you cannot check both of the immediately following boxes in relation to any person to whom the notice was sent by e-mail, fax or other electronic means, because he or she has not provided the required acknowledgement, you must re-deliver the notice and Rule 25-2(1)(b) documents by mail or personal delivery and swear to that delivery under the first or second of the boxes in this section 2.]

[ ]   Each of the persons who received delivery by e-mail, fax or other electronic means has, in writing, acknowledged receipt of the document(s) referred to in this section.

[ ]   I will retain a copy of those acknowledgements until the personal representative of the deceased is discharged and will produce those acknowledgements promptly after being requested to do so by the registrar.

SWORN (OR AFFIRMED)	)
BEFORE ME at *[location]*,	)
British Columbia,	)
on *[month, day, year]*.	)
	)
	)
_____	) _____
A commissioner for taking affidavits	) DEPONENT'S NAME
for British Columbia	)

Nicole Garton, LLB, TEP

Form P10 (Rule 25-3(2))

This is the 1st affidavit
of *[name]* in this case and was
made on *[month, day, year]*

No.
Vancouver Registry

In the Supreme Court of British Columbia

In the Matter of the Estate of *[legal name of deceased]*, deceased

AFFIDAVIT OF ASSETS AND LIABILITIES FOR DOMICILED ESTATE GRANT

I, *[name]*, of *[address]*, *[occupation]*, SWEAR (OR AFFIRM) THAT:

1 I am an applicant for a grant of probate in relation to the estate of *[legal name of deceased]* (the "deceased").

2 I have made a diligent search and inquiry to find the property and liabilities of the deceased.

3 Attached to this affidavit as Exhibit A is a Statement of Assets, Liabilities and Distribution that discloses

    (a) all of the property of the deceased, irrespective of its location, nature or value, that passes to the applicant in the applicant's capacity as the deceased's personal representative,

    (b) the value of that property, and

    (c) the liabilities that charge or encumber that property.

4 If I determine that there is any property or liability that has not been disclosed in Exhibit A, or that information contained in this affidavit is incorrect or incomplete, I will promptly after learning of the same file an affidavit of assets and liabilities in Form P14 to disclose the correct and complete information.

5 In addition to the probate fees payable in relation to any property disclosed in Exhibit A, I promise to pay the Minister of Finance the probate fees payable with respect to the value of any property that passes to me as the deceased's personal

representative, and that is not disclosed in Exhibit A, on a determination being made as to the value of that asset.

SWORN (OR AFFIRMED)	)	
BEFORE ME at *[location]*,	)	
British Columbia,	)	
on *[month, day, year]*	)	
	)	
	)	
_____	)	_____
A commissioner for taking affidavits	)	DEPONENT'S NAME
for British Columbia	)	

This is Exhibit A referred to in the
affidavit of *[name]* sworn
(or affirmed) before me on *[month, day, year]*.

_____

A commissioner for taking affidavits
for British Columbia

In the matter of the Estate of *[legal name]*, Deceased

STATEMENT OF ASSETS, LIABILITIES & DISTRIBUTION

Part 1 **Real Property** (including mortgages and vendors' and purchasers' interests in agreements for sale)	Within or Without British Columbia	Value at Death
Civic Address of property: Registered in the name of: Parcel Identifier: Legal Description: Appraised by: Appraised value:	Within	$
TOTAL:		$
Part II **Personal Property** (all assets except real property)	Within or Without British Columbia	Value at Death
A. Tangible Personal Property (1) Personal property, clothing and household effects No commercial value B. Intangible Personal Property		$ 0.00

1)			
2)			
	TOTAL:	$	
	GROSS VALUE OF ESTATE:	**$**	

Part III Liabilities	Paid or Unpaid	Amount
Unsecured Liabilities		
Secured Liabilities		
TOTAL:	**$**	

Chapter 9

Where There's No Will... There's Still a Way

Introduction

When a person dies without a will, they are said to have died intestate. With no will to dictate distribution of the deceased's estate, one must look to WESA for direction on how the property of the deceased will flow. There is also the possibility of a "partial intestacy", where there is a valid will, but it does not deal with all of the property of the deceased. The property that is not dealt with in the will has to flow by way of WESA.

If there is no will, a person who is in a position to handle the deceased's assets may apply to the court for a representation grant to become an administrator of the estate. The person who applies is typically a spouse, relative, or friend of the deceased, and may be applying with the consent of other potential beneficiaries. In some cases, the court might insist that the person applying get an insurance bond or provide some security. This may happen if one of the parties is not capable of handling his or her affairs and does not have a representative, or if one of the parties asks the court to order security (WESA, s. 128). This security protects the estate beneficiaries in case the personal representative mishandles the estate assets.

The way the property will be divided depends on what family or next-of-kin the deceased left living at the date of death. The chart at the end of this chapter shows the "Parentelic Distribution" scheme that WESA brought into effect. This scheme provides that the closest family to the parent will inherit rather than the closest to the grandparent. The degrees of separation stop after the fourth degree, so if there is no kinship that is at least four degrees from the deceased, then the estate will pass to the Crown.

Under intestacy law, there is a prescribed amount that a spouse will inherit. If there are children that the spouse and the deceased had together, then the spouse will receive $300,000 plus half of the residue (or remainder) of the estate. If there were children of the deceased who are not also the surviving spouse's children, then the spouse will receive the sum of $150,000 plus half of the residue of the estate. This is a change that WESA brought into effect. Previously, the surviving spouse would only be entitled to the first

$65,000 and a life interest in the family residence. Under WESA, on top of the $300,000 (or $150,000) and half the residue, the surviving spouse also has the option to purchase the spousal home within 180 days from the date that the estate grant is made.

Missing Intestate Successors

It is not always easy to locate every intestate successor, and you may find that you are simply unable to obtain an address for someone who is entitled to notice of the proposed estate grant application. In this case, you may make an application to the Supreme Court to dispense with the notice requirement by advising the court that their location is unknown, under Supreme Court Civil Rule 25-2(14).

The applicant must make "reasonable efforts" to find the person, including inquiries with family, searching registries and online information, reviewing social media, vital statistics or voter registration, etc. You will need to swear an affidavit that sets out exactly the measures taken in trying to locate the person. There is a high threshold to ensure that you have attempted to locate the missing person, so you may need to explain all the avenues used. It might be prudent in your circumstances to hire a skip tracer to see if they are able to find the missing intestate successor. If the court is satisfied with your efforts, they will issue you an order that eliminates the requirement to send notice to that missing person.

Bonds

Sometimes the court will see fit for the administrator of an estate to post bond. This is a security measure for circumstances where there might be minor beneficiaries or mentally incompetent beneficiaries, or where a beneficiary requests a bond by applying to the Supreme Court. The point of the bond is to protect the assets of the estate. This only applies on an intestacy, since the person who is applying for the estate grant has not been nominated by the deceased. The amount of the bond is usually the same as the value of the beneficiaries' share of the estate. The bond represents insurance from the administrator that the beneficiaries will receive their share of the estate and that the administrator cannot run off with the assets that pass through the estate. It is typically renewed annually until the estate has been wound up.

If you are required to post a bond, they can usually be obtained through insurance companies. It is very important to make sure that you are bondable before proceeding with the estate grant application.

Estate Grant Application

Without a will, the estate grant application is called a Grant of Administration Without Will Annexed. Because there is no will appointing an executor, someone needs to step up to make the estate grant application and administer the estate. See Chapter 2 for a listing of section 130 of WESA that sets out the priority among applicants that can apply to the court to obtain the authority to administer the estate. If you are part of the list of available applicants, but there are people living that have a prior entitlement to apply before you, it is prudent to obtain their consent before you apply for the estate grant. The signed consents that you obtain do not need to be filed in the court registry with your application, but it is best practice to keep them on file in case you need to rely on them later on.

The application for an estate grant is now governed by Rule 25-3. A standard (simple) application for a grant of administration without will annexed include the following prescribed forms:

- P1—Notice of proposed application in relation to estate;

- P2—Submission for estate grant;

- P5—Affidavit of application for grant of probate;

- P9—Affidavit of delivery;

- P10—Affidavit of assets and liabilities for domiciled estate grant.

In addition, an application for estate grant should include the original will (if applicable) and the results of the Search for Wills Notice issued by the Vital Statistics Agency, in duplicate, and poss bly a letter from the Public Guardian and Trustee if required.

It may be helpful for you to review the pre-grant estate administration checklist produced at the end of Chapter 8 to help keep you organized.

Form P1 Notice of Proposed Application in Relation to Estate

With the introduct on of WESA into provincial law, the notice requirements shifted noticeably. The administrator without will annexed must figure out who is entitled to notice in accordance with section 121 of WESA, which states:

121   (1)   An applicant for a grant of probate or administration must give notice of the proposed application to the persons referred to in the Supreme Court Civil Rules.

         (2)   An applicant or personal representative who, in accordance with the Supreme Court Civil Rules, makes reasonable efforts to discover the existence, identity or whereabouts of persons to whom the notice under subsection (1) is required to be given, but is unsuccessful, is not liable for any loss or damage arising from not giving the required notice except for claims to recover property or enforce an order under Division 6 of Part 4.

Section 25-2 of the Supreme Court Civil Rules expresses who is entitled to notice:

(1) Subject to this rule, unless the court otherwise orders, a person intending to apply for an estate grant or for the resealing of a foreign grant in relation to this estate of a deceased must, at least 21 days before submitting for filing the materials required for that application under this Part, deliver the following to the persons referred to in subrule (2):

a. A notice that complies with subrule (3);

b. Whichever of the following, if any, that applies to the intended application:

    i. If the intended applicant intends to apply for a grant of probate or a grant of administration with will annexed, a copy of the will in relation to which the application is to be made;

    ii. If the intended applicant intends to apply for the resealing of a foreign grant or for an ancillary grant of probate or an ancillary grant of administration with will annexed, a copy of the foreign grant and, if the copy of the will in relation to which the foreign grant was issued is not attached to the foreign grant, a copy of the will;

    iii. If the intended applicant intends to apply for an ancillary grant of administration without will annexed, a copy of the foreign grant.

(2) The documents referred to in subrule (1) must be delivered to the following persons:

a. If the deceased left a will, each of the following who is not a person by whom or on whose behalf the documents referred to in subrule (1) are to be delivered (a person by whom or on whose behalf the documents referred to in subrule (1) are to be delivered is, in this subrule, called an "intended applicant"):

    i. Each person

        A. Who is named in the will as executor or alternate executor,

        B. Whose right to make an application for an estate grant in relation to the deceased is prior to or equal to the

> intended applicant's right to make that application, and
>
> C.   Who is alive at the time of the deceased's death;
>
> ii.   Each beneficiary under the will who is not referred to in subparagraph (1) of this paragraph;
>
> iii. Each person who, under Division 1 of Part 3 of the *Wills, Estates and Succession Act,* would have been an intestate successor if the deceased did not leave a will and who is not referred to in subparagraph (i) or (ii) of this paragraph;
>
> **b.   If the deceased did not leave a will,**
>
> **i.   Each person who, under Division 1 of Part 3 of the *Wills, Estates and Succession Act,* is an intestate successor of the deceased, and**
>
> **ii. Each creditor of the deceased whose claim exceeds $10,000 and who is not referred to in subparagraph (i) of this paragraph;**
>
> c.   If the deceased was a Nisga'a citizen, the Nisga'a Lisims government;
>
> d.   If the deceased was a member of a treaty first nation, the treaty first nation;
>
> e.   Any other person who, by court order under subrule (14)(a) is to receive notice;
>
> f.   Any person not referred to in paragraph (a), (b), (c), (d) or (e) of this subrule who has served a citation on the intended applicant in relation to the deceased.
>
> **(Emphasis added)**

All of the appropriate people need to be mailed the P1 Notice. As a general rule, all the intestate successors must receive the P1 Notice. Because of this rule, it is best practice to wait until you have received the results of the Search for a Wills Notice before you send out any notices to anyone, in case a will is found.

There is the option to deliver the P1 Notice by email or fax; however, it is best practice to send it by regular mail. The reason for this is, if you send the package electronically, the court will require the recipient to acknowledge (usually by return email) that they have received it. The personal representative must then retain the email acknowledgement of the delivery of the notice until they are discharged as executor. If the person being provided with the notice does not acknowledge delivery, the personal representative will need to mail the P1 notice to them regardless; therefore, it is easier to mail it in first instance. The package is deemed to be "delivered" on the date that it is mailed. You will eventually need to swear an affidavit that will be filed with the estate grant application package attesting to mailing the P1 Notice, the date it was mailed on, and who it was mailed to.

It is important to note the date of mailing, as the personal representative must wait 21 days after mailing the Notice before they will be allowed to file the rest of the estate grant application package to the Probate Registry. This 21-day waiting period allows anyone that received notice of the proposed application the opportunity to oppose the application, which they can do by filing a Notice of Dispute.

There are some common issues that may arise when delivering the P1 Notice:

Minors
Delivery must be made to the minor's parents if the minor lives with all parents, or to the parent or guardian who has the responsibility for financial decisions relating to the minor. Otherwise, the notice should be delivered to each of the addresses where the minor resides. See section 182 of WESA.

In addition to serving the minor's parent(s) or guardian(s), the personal representative also must serve the Notice upon the Public Guardian and Trustee of British Columbia, unless:

- The minor is not a spouse or a child of the deceased.

Mentally incompetent persons
Delivery must be made to the Committee (does not include an attorney appointed under a Power of Attorney or a representative under a Representation Agreement) of the mentally incompetent person as well as to the Public Guardian and Trustee of British Columbia. If there is no Committee, then the Notice is sent to the mentally incompetent person and the Public Guardian and Trustee of British Columbia.

If you are unsure if a person is mentally incompetent or not, all notices should be given out of an abundance of caution.

Missing persons
See explanation of missing intestate successors earlier in this chapter.

Deceased beneficiaries
If the intestate successor predeceased the deceased, WESA provisions apply regarding alternate beneficiaries and notice then goes to those persons. See section 46(1) of WESA.

If the intestate successor died after the deceased, notice should be given to the personal representative of the deceased intestate successor, as the gift will pass to the deceased intestate successor's estate.

If notice is required to be sent to the Public Guardian and Trustee, you must include, in addition to the standard P1 Notice, a further notice in writing that sets out the additional information required under Rule 25-1(13):

(13)   At the time that a notice is delivered to the Public Guardian and Trustee under subrule (8) or (11), the intended applicant must also deliver to the Public Guardian and Trustee a notice, in writing, setting out

    (a)   The name of every other person to whom notice is required to be delivered under subrule (8) or (11), and

    (b)   The most recent of each of the following that is known to the intended applicant about each of those persons:

        (i)   The person's residential address, inside or outside British Columbia;

        (ii)   The person's postal address, inside or outside British Columbia;

        (iii)   The person's e-mail address, and;

        (iv)   The person's fax number.

Note that if delivery of the P1 Notice is required on the Public Guardian and Trustee, the Public Guardian and Trustee must be given opportunity to respond, and the applicant must submit the written comments of the Public Guardian and Trustee to the court along with the application for the estate grant. The Public Guardian and Trustee must also be provided with copies of the filed application documents promptly after filing them. When you issue the filed documents to the Public Guardian and Trustee, you will also need to include a certified cheque or a bank draft in the amount of $336 (as of the date of this printing) made payable to the Public Guardian and Trustee of British Columbia, as they require payment for reviewing the application on behalf of a minor or mentally incompetent beneficiary.

In any estate where notice to the Public Guardian and Trustee is required, ensure that notice is properly prepared and delivered and that all relevant information is included. Failure to properly deliver notice in the form required could necessitate the notice having to be resent, and the 21-day waiting period restarted.

A sample P1 Notice is included at the end of this chapter for your review.

Form P2 Submission for Estate Grant

The Submission for Estate Grant will be the document that initiates the estate grant proceeding. It sets out certain information about the deceased and the applicant, and the nature of the grant that is being sought.

The top part of the form is called the "style of cause" and it shows only the full legal name of the deceased (no known aliases included). Any aliases will be listed in Part 1 of the Submission for Estate Grant where indicated.

At the top right-hand corner of every document, the style of cause states the court file number and the location of the court registry. At this point in time, since no documents have been filed with the court registry, there is no court number to include. When you file the documents in court, the registry will stamp your documents with the file number that is assigned to your matter. The style of cause must be consistent on every document that you prepare that will be filed in the application process.

The "applicant" to be named on the first line of page one of the Submission for Estate Grant should be the personal representative. The P2 was designed using a check-box format to address the fact that a large number of applicants commencing probate applications do not have legal counsel and are therefore self-represented. Each numbered paragraph of the Submission for Estate Grant has multiple options and those that are not selected should be deleted from the form; however, your submission will not be rejected by the court registry if you do *not* delete the sections that you are not including. Words within the standard paragraph being selected should not be deleted or changed if at all possible.

There are two different types of applications that you could be making with the P2 Submission for Estate Grant. The first one is a grant of administration without will annexed. For this to be granted, you must have enough information to swear the Affidavit of Assets and Liabilities in Form P10. This means that you have contacted all of the financial institutions and they have provided the balances as of the date of death for the deceased, and that you have already been advised of all of the deceased's known assets and liabilities to the extent that the personal representative can swear is a complete listing. If you are missing even one account balance, you will not be able to obtain the estate grant.

The second type of application you can make with the P2 Submission for Estate Grant is what is called an Authorization to Obtain Estate Information, in Form P18. This is required if you do not have enough information to swear the Affidavit of Assets and Liabilities. See the section Form P10 Affidavit of Assets and Liabilities later in this chapter for more information on Form P18.

On the first page of the P2 Submission, you have the option to ask the court to provide you with any number of court-certified copies of the estate grant or the Statement of Assets, Liabilities and Distribution. As a general practice, you should get one court-certified copy for each financial institution or organization where the deceased held assets (such as the Land Title Office or ICBC). That way, when go to transfer the assets into your name as personal representative, you can provide each institution with a court-certified copy for their records. For Land Title purposes, you will need a court-certified copy of the estate grant in addition to a court-certified copy of the Statement of Assets and Liabilities and Distribution.

The probate registry will keep the original estate grant and only provides the personal representative with a copy, or court-certified copy. Therefore, if you need to certify or notarize a copy at a later date, a lawyer or a notary cannot certify that they have seen the original, but only a copy. This is why it is best practice to obtain a number of court-certified copies from the court registry, though they will charge you extra fees to do so.

Note that when completing the appropriate Schedule to the Submission for Estate Grant, the term "n/a" will not be accepted by the registry. If there is no person who meets the criteria of a particular category, simply write "none".

If there are other documents being filed with the application, these documents should be listed in paragraph 7 of the Submission for Estate Grant.

A sample P2 Submission for Estate Grant is included at the end of this chapter.

Form P5 Affidavit of Applicant for Grant of Administration Without Will Annexed

This affidavit is sworn by the personal representative applying for the estate grant. Keep in mind that this is a sworn document, and therefore needs to be "sworn" in front of a lawyer, notary, or commissioner for taking oaths and affidavits for British Columbia.

The affidavit is also a check-box form to fill in. It confirms the personal representative's relationship to the deceased under section 130 of WESA, that they did a diligent and complete search for a will or testamentary document but could not find any, and that they believe there is no will of the deceased.

A sample Form P5 is included at the end of this chapter.

In the case of multiple applicants, there are three ways to proceed:

1. One applicant can sign the P5, and the other(s) can sign the Form P8 (Affidavit in Support) – preferred method;

2. Both applicants can sign the same P5 form; or

3. Each applicant can sign a separate P5 form.

A sample Form P8 is included at the end of this chapter.

Form P9 Affidavit of Delivery

An Affidavit of Delivery in Form P9 is required to be sworn and submitted with the estate administration application. This form confirms with the court registry that the appropriate notices have been forwarded and delivered to the appropriate persons (see earlier in this chapter for more on Form P1 Notices). The Form P1 Notice that was issued to all these people needs to be attached to the end of the Affidavit of Delivery to demonstrate what was sent out.

If the personal representative is the person who actually put the P1 Notice in the mail box to send out, then the personal representative should be the one to swear the Affidavit of Delivery. If someone else mailed these documents on behalf of the personal representative, then this person should be the one to swear the Affidavit of Delivery.

In the body of the Affidavit of Delivery, you will list the name, address, and relationship to the deceased for each recipient of the Notice. Ensure that you include the date that you mailed the Notice to each person so that the registry can make sure that you have waited the requisite 21 days before submitting the application.

A sample Form P9 Affidavit of Delivery is included at the end of this chapter.

Form P10 Affidavit of Assets and Liabilities

The Affidavit of Assets and Liabilities is designed to set out to the court all of the assets and liabilities of the estate. The affidavit has an exhibit attached to it called the "Statement of Assets, Liabilities and Distribution" (SALD). The SALD is a form based on regulations passed under the *Probate Fee Act,* (SBC 1999, c 4.); however, it is important to note that the "Distribution" heading under the title is no longer a requirement. WESA changed the requirements so that only the assets and liabilities of the estate are required to be listed. You will need to set out all property of the deceased, irrespective of their nature, location, or value, that passes to the personal representative for distribution among the beneficiaries.

The P10 is the form that is used when the deceased was ordinarily resident in British Columbia. If the deceased was not ordinarily resident in British Columbia and all the property outside of British Columbia has or will be administered by a foreign personal representative, Form P11 would be used instead of the P10.

This affidavit is used by the court to determine how much in probate fees is payable by the estate.

The affidavit confirms that you are the applicant for the estate grant and that you have done a complete and diligent search for all property and debts of the deceased. It further confirms that, if you happen to come across any other property of the deceased that was not included in your sworn statement, you will immediately fill out a Supplemental Affidavit of Assets and Liabilities and file it with the court registry so that the court can reassess the amount of probate fees payable. Finally, it confirms that you will pay the probate fees as assessed by the probate registry.

The Form P10 and its exhibit requires the disclosure of the following:

- All property of the deceased that passes to the personal representative;

- The location of that property;

- The value of that property; and

- Any liabilities that encumber that property.

Note again that if there is property that is held in joint tenancy with a right of survivorship, the surviving joint tenant receives that property outright and that property does not need to be disclosed on the Form P10 and SALD unless it is being held in a bare trust on behalf of someone else, but that is beyond the scope of these materials.

Also, as previously mentioned, if there is a registered account such as an RRSP, RRIF, or a life insurance policy that names a specific designated beneficiary, that property does not pass to the estate, it passes directly to the specified beneficiary and therefore is not included in the SALD.

You are not allowed to put any unknowns in the SALD. Under the old rules, you could put a "to be determined" for a value that you could not obtain readily; however, with the change in law, the court registry will no longer allow this except in very rare circumstances, such as if there was a pending class action law suit settlement that had yet to be distributed where it is impossible to know how much money the deceased will eventually receive. Furthermore, you are not allowed to use the term "n/a", and instead must use the term "None" or "Nil" if the deceased did not possess those types of property.

If you are unable to obtain all the requisite information to fill out the P10 in its entirety, then you may need to first ask the court registry to issue you an Authorization to Obtain Estate Information, in Form P18, before obtaining the estate grant. This authorization is issued when you have submitted all other probate application materials to the court with the exception of the P10 Affidavit and exhibit. The probate registry will provide you with the filed Authorization which you can then send to any financial institution or organization that has not provided you with the information that you need to obtain the date of death balances for all assets and liabilities of the deceased. The institution then is required to provide you with this information within 30 days of receiving the Authorization.

Once you have received the information, you can fill in the Affidavit and SALD, swear that affidavit and submit it to the court where it joins the rest of the estate grant application materials, and then a grant can be issued if everything is in order.

As mentioned above, in the instance that the personal representative discovers an asset or liability that they were not aware of when they filed the P10 and the SALD, they will need to submit a Supplemental Affidavit in form P14 to disclose to the court the other assets or liabilities that should have been included in the P10.

Statement of Assets, Liabilities and Distribution

Part I: Real Property

> Real property refers to land, and includes any mortgages or registered encumbrances. If there is no real property owned by the deceased, then indicate "none" in this section, but do not leave it blank.
>
> When you do your information gathering to determine the assets of the estate, you should perform a title search of the Land Title Office registry (you can go to the actual registry, or you may order the title search online using an online account, for a fee). This document will provide you with the particulars of the information needed for the SALD. The title search will list the owners and their full legal names (make sure you have this name in your Wills Notice Search and listed in your aliases in the P2 Submission document). It will tell you how the property is owned: whether the deceased was the sole owner, whether they owned the property as joint tenants (if the surviving joint tenant is alive, the real property will not be listed on the SALD), or whether they owned the property as tenants in common (they may be tenants as to an undivided half interest, or as other percentage

interests, and this needs to be expressed on the SALD. You will only state the value of the deceased's interest in the property). If there is more than one owner on the title search, if the title search does not expressly state "as joint tenants", and if it is silent on how much of an interest is owned by each owner, the default presumption is that the title is held as tenants in common in equal shares.

You will need the Parcel Identifier Number or "PID", which is a 9-digit number, as well as the "legal description" of the interest in property, and the civic address of the property. You will also need to have the BC Property Assessment value for the current year so that you can state on the SALD how much the property is worth. Alternatively, you can obtain an appraisal from a property appraiser or obtain the market value from a real estate agent. Be careful if you are just listing the BC Property Assessment value, as it might be significantly different from the market value, depending on various factors. Note that if you only disclose the assessed value and then end up selling the property for a lot more than what was stated on the SALD, you might open up the estate to a capital gains charge, taxable at the deceased's marginal tax rate.

Once you have stated the value of the property, you can then deduct any registered mortgage listed on title, from the gross value of the property. You need to ensure that you have the exact amount owing as of the date of death. You cannot use a standard bank statement for this purpose and must contact the financial institution to find out exactly what the balance was from the date of death.

Part II: Personal Property

All of the other assets of the deceased, <u>as of the date of death</u>, must be listed in this section. This includes tangible (collections, art, vehicles, etc.) and intangible (bank accounts, investments, stocks and bonds or other securities, etc.) property.

Tangible property will include household possessions, but these generally have no real commercial value. Of course, there are exceptions but if nothing is particularly valuable, then you can state that household possessions have a "nil" value as of the date of death, or a "nominal" value, which counted as zero balance towards the gross value of the estate. Furniture can be given a value estimate based on what it might be worth at a garage sale. If the furniture was held jointly and passed to the surviving joint tenant, you can list that in the statement as well.

In any event, you may want to retain the services of a qualified appraiser if there are unique valuables or any possessions whose value you are unsure of.

Ensure that you have done a complete and diligent search of the papers and files of the deceased to make completely sure that you include everything that the deceased owned as of the date of death. Note that for accounts and intangible property you cannot use monthly statements to provide the balance, but must acquire the exact value as of the date of death and be sure to include any accrued interest to the date of death if an account is interest-bearing.

Any death benefits or issuances from Old Age Security or the Canada Pension Plan for the month of death should be included in the statement. Veteran's benefits are included but be cautioned that survivor's benefits are not included.

If the deceased owned an insurance policy or a pension that did not list a designated beneficiary, the proceeds will fall to the estate. You will need to include all information known about the policy or pension in the Statement.

There is no longer any need to list a safety deposit box in the personal property section; however, if there are contents of value in the safety deposit box, those need to be included.

Note that intangible assets, such as bank accounts and investments, are generally deemed to be 'within' British Columbia even if the branch location is outside of British Columbia and therefore are subject to probate fees.

Part III: Liabilities

All debts or accounts payable as of the date of death need to be listed in this section. You need to include whether the debt has been paid or if it remains unpaid. Before any assets of the estate are distributed to any intestate successor, all of the debts listed need to be paid.

You can notify the creditors of the death of the deceased and ensure that you obtain outstanding balance as of the date of death from them. You can advise creditors that they will need to wait to be paid until you receive the estate grant and have access to the accounts. Some creditors will halt the interest from accruing from the date of death, and some will not.

The accounts of the deceased will usually be frozen until such time as an estate grant is received. However, the bank will usually issue a cheque for the funeral expenses and will issue a bank draft for probate fees, but you need to produce the amount owing on each for them to issue the correct amount.

The probate registry only requires you to list liabilities that charge or encumber a specific item of property (like a mortgage), or if there is a creditor that has a claim that is over $10,000 (as they essentially become a beneficiary of the estate).

A sample Form P10 and SALD is included at the end of this chapter.

Parentelic Distribution under Section 23 of the *Wills, Estates and Succession Act*

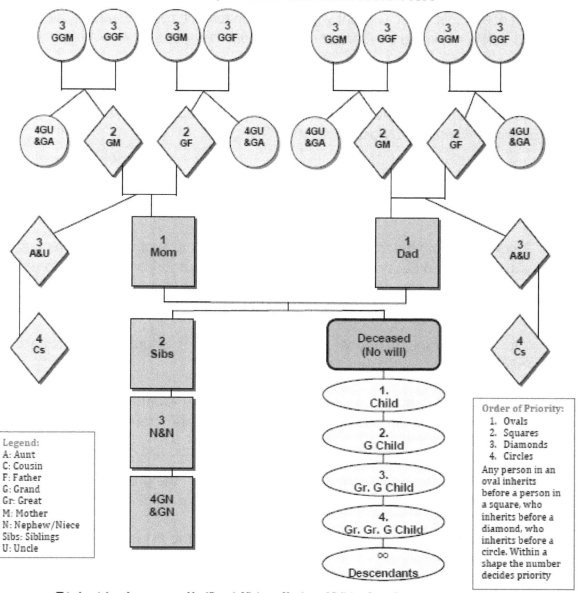

This chart is based on one created by Alberta's Ministry of Justice and Solicitor General.

The *Wills, Estates and Succession Act* came into force on March 31, 2014. This document was developed by the Ministry of Justice to support the transition to the *Wills, Estates and Succession Act*. It is not legal advice and should not be relied upon for those purposes.

Form P1 (Rule 25-2(3))

NOTICE OF PROPOSED APPLICATION IN RELATION TO ESTATE

TAKE NOTICE THAT:

The applicant(s) *[name of applicant(s)]* propose(s) to apply, in the Vancouver court registry, for a grant of administration without will annexed in relation to the estate of the deceased described below who died on *[date of death–month, day, year]*.

Full legal name of deceased: *[first name] [middle name(s)] [last name/family name]*

Last residential address of the deceased: *[Include street number or post office box, city/ town, province, country and postal code.]*

    [X]   This application does not relate to a will.

AND TAKE NOTICE THAT:

(1)   Before obtaining the foregoing grant or resealing, the applicant may be granted an authorization to obtain estate information or an authorization to obtain resealing information, as the case may be, in relation to that grant or resealing for the purposes of obtaining financial information in relation to the grant or resealing.

(2)   You have a right to oppose, by filing a notice of dispute in accordance with Rule 25-10(1),

    (a)   if the intended application is for an estate grant, the granting of either or both of an authorization to obtain estate information and the estate grant, or

    (b)   if the intended application is for a resealing, the granting of either or both of an authorization to obtain resealing information and the resealing.

(3)   You may or may not be entitled to claim against the estate for relief, including a claim under

    (a)   the *Family Law Act*, or

    (b)   Division 6 of Part 4 of the *Wills, Estates and Succession Act*.

(4)   If you choose to take a step referred to in paragraph (2) or (3), you must do so within the time limited by any relevant rule of court or other enactment.

The Heritage Trust Estate Administration Boot Camp

(5)   You may consult with your own lawyer concerning your interest in, or rights against, the estate.

(6)   After the applicant has filed a submission for estate grant or submission for resealing, you may apply for an order requiring the applicant to provide security unless the applicant is the Public Guardian and Trustee. Filing a notice of dispute will prevent a grant from being issued before you are able to apply for the order requiring security.

(7)   An authorization to obtain estate information, an authorization to obtain resealing information or a grant may issue to the applicant, or a foreign grant may be resealed, on any date that is _at least 21 days_ after the date on which this notice is delivered to you or on any earlier date ordered by the court.

(8)   If an authorization to obtain estate information issues to the applicant, the applicant may apply for a grant without further notice. If an authorization to obtain resealing information issues to the applicant, the applicant may apply for the resealing of the foreign grant without further notice to you.

(9)   If a grant issues to the applicant, the applicant must provide, if there is a will, to the beneficiaries or, if there is no will, to intestate successors of the deceased, an accounting as to how the estate was administered and how the estate assets were distributed, and if a foreign grant is resealed as a result of the application, the intended applicant must provide, if there is a will, to the beneficiaries or, if there is no will, to intestate successors of the deceased, an accounting as to how the estate comprising the assets to which the resealed grant applies was administered and how those assets were distributed.

[If this notice of proposed application is required to be delivered to the Public Guardian and Trustee under Rule 25-2, ensure all additional information required under Rule 25-2(13) is provided to the Public Guardian and Trustee.]

INFORMATION ABOUT EACH APPLICANT

[Complete the following for each applicant. Add additional sheets as required.]

Name: _[first name] [middle name(s)] [last name/family name]_

Mailing address: _[Include street number or post office box, city/town, province, country and postal code.]_

[Check whichever one of the immediately following 2 boxes is correct.]

[ ]   This applicant is not an individual

[ ]   This applicant is an individual and ordinarily lives

[If you checked the second of the immediately preceding 2 boxes, check whichever one of the immediately following 2 boxes is correct and provide any required information.]

[ ]   at the mailing address noted above

[ ]   in the following city and country: *[specify]*

ADDRESS FOR SERVICE OF APPLICANT

[X]   The applicant's address for service is

Street address for service:

Fax number address for service (if any):

E-mail address for service (if any):

Telephone number:

Date: *[dd/mmm/yyyy]*

_____

Signature of
[ ]   lawyer for applicant
[ ]   applicant

[type or print name]

Form P2 (Rule 25-3(2))

No.
Vancouver Registry

In the Supreme Court of British Columbia

In the Matter of the Estate of *[legal name of deceased]*, deceased

SUBMISSION FOR ESTATE GRANT

This submission for estate grant is submitted on behalf of: *[name(s) of applicant(s)]*.

I, *[name of applicant]*, am applying for the following in relation to the estate of the deceased described in Part 1 of this submission for estate grant (the "deceased"):

[X]   Grant of administration without will annexed

[Check whichever one of the immediately following 2 boxes is correct.]

[ ]   I am/We are submitting with this submission for estate grant an affidavit of assets and liabilities in Form P10 or P11 and therefore do not require an authorization to obtain estate information.

[ ]   I am/We are seeking an authorization to obtain estate information so that I/ we can secure the information necessary to prepare and submit an affidavit of assets and liabilities for estate grant.

[X]   I request *[number of copies]* court-certified copies of the estate grant. *and 1 court-certified copy of the Statement of Assets, Liabilities & Distribution.

[ ]   I request *[number of copies]* court-certified copies of the authorization to obtain estate information.

This submission for estate grant has 4 Parts:

Part 1: Information about the Deceased

Part 2: Contact Information for the Applicant(s)

Part 3: Documents Filed with this submission for estate grant

Part 4: Schedule

Date: *[dd/mm/yyyy]*

_____

Signature of *[lawyer]*

[x]   lawyer for applicant(s)

[ ]   applicant

[type or print name]

Part 1: INFORMATION ABOUT THE DECEASED

Full legal name of deceased: *[first name]*, *[middle name(s)]*, *[last name/family name]*

Other names in which the deceased held or may have held an interest in property:

1

2

3

Last residential address of the deceased:

      Street number and street name: *[specify]*
      OR Post office box: *[specify]*
      City/Town: *[specify]*
      Province: *[specify]*
      Country: *[specify]*
      Postal Code: *[specify]*

Deceased's date of death: *[month, day, year]*

[Check whichever one of the immediately following 3 boxes is correct and provide any required information.]

    [ ]   The deceased was neither a Nisga'a citizen nor a member of a treaty first nation.

    [ ]   The deceased was a Nisga'a citizen.

    [ ]   The deceased was a member of the *[name]* treaty first nation.

Part 2: CONTACT INFORMATION FOR THE APPLICANT(S)

      Street address for service:

The Heritage Trust Estate Administration Boot Camp

Fax number address for service (if any):

E-mail address for service (if any):

Telephone number:

Part 3: DOCUMENTS FILED WITH THIS SUBMISSION FOR ESTATE GRANT

1 |*[Check whichever one of the immediately following 2 boxes is correct and file the specified affidavit(s).]*

    [X]   There is one applicant to this submission for estate grant and

        (a)   the applicant has made an affidavit in Form *[Select whichever one of the following 5 choices is correct—P3/P4/P5/P6/P7]*, and

        (b)   that affidavit is filed with this submission for estate grant.

    [ ]   There are 2 or more applicants to this submission for estate grant and

        (a)   at least one of the applicants has made an affidavit in Form [Select whichever one of the following 5 choices is correct—P5/P6/P7],

        (b)   that affidavit is filed with this submission for estate grant, and

        (c)   the remaining applicant(s) has/have made (an) affidavit(s) in Form P8 and that/those affidavit(s) is/are filed with this submission for estate grant.

2   [X]   Filed with this submission for estate grant is the following Affidavit of Delivery in Form P9 that confirms that the documents referred to in Rule 25-2 were delivered to all of the persons to whom, under that rule, the documents were required to be delivered:

        Affidavit of *[name]* sworn *[month, day, year]*

    [ ]   No affidavit of delivery is attached. In accordance with Rule 25-2, no one, other than the applicant(s), is entitled to notice.

3   Filed with this submission for estate grant are 2 copies of the certificate of the chief executive officer under the Vital Statistics Act indicating the results of a search for a wills notice filed by or on behalf of the deceased.

4   [X]   This application is for a grant of administration without will annexed.

5   This application is for a grant of administration without will annexed or an ancillary grant of administration without will annexed.

6   [X]   This application is for a grant of administration without will annexed or an ancillary grant of administration without will annexed.

7   [X]   No documents other than those described elsewhere in this submission for estate grant are filed with this submission for estate grant.

7   [X]   In addition to the documents described elsewhere in this submission for estate grant, the following documents are filed with this submission for estate grant:

1

2

3

8   [X]   All documents filed with this submission for estate grant are written in the English language.

Part 4: SCHEDULE

1   [X]   Attached to this submission for estate grant is a Schedule for Grant of Administration without Will Annexed.

SCHEDULE FOR GRANT OF ADMINISTRATION
WITHOUT WILL ANNEXED

1   Listed in each of the following paragraphs is every person who falls within the class of persons identified by that paragraph:

[Provide under each of the following paragraphs the full name of each person to whom the paragraph applies, whether or not that person is named elsewhere in this submission for estate grant.]

[List each named person on a separate line.]

(a)   spouse, if any, of the deceased *[see section 2 of the Wills, Estates and Succession Act] [Provide the appropriate response(s), as applicable: spouse [provide name of spouse]/no currently living spouse as defined by section 2 of the Wills, Estates and Succession Act [provide name of spouse and indicate "(deceased)"]/other former spouse(s) [provide name(s) of other former spouse(s) and indicate "(former spouse)"]/never married.]: [specify]*

(b)   child(ren), if any, of the deceased *[Provide the appropriate response(s), as applicable: living child(ren) of deceased [provide name(s) of child(ren)]/any child(ren) of the deceased who died before the deceased [provide name(s) of child(ren) and indicate "(deceased)"]/no children.]: [specify]*

(c)   each person, if any, not named in paragraph (a) or (b), who is entitled to receive all or part of the estate of a person who dies without a will: *[see section 23 of the Wills, Estates and Succession Act] [List all living persons who would be entitled on intestacy and their relationship to the deceased.]: [specify]*

Note: The foregoing wording for paragraph (c) is that set out in Form P2 in Appendix A.1 of the Civil Rules. However, it is suggested that the following wording is more appropriate:

"each person, if any, not named in paragraph (a) or (b), who is an intestate successor of the deceased".

(d)   each creditor of the deceased, if any, not named in paragraph (a), (b) or (c) whose claim exceeds $10 000: *[specify]*

(e)   each citor, if any, not named in paragraph (a), (b), (c) or (d) *[see Rule 25-11] [List anyone who has filed a citation or indicate that no citation has been received.]: [specify]*

Nicole Garton, LLB, TEP

Form P5 (Rule 25-3(2))

This is the 1st affidavit
of *[name]* in this case and was
made on *[month, day, year]*

No.
Vancouver Registry

In the Supreme Court of British Columbia

In the Matter of the Estate of *[legal name of deceased]*, deceased

AFFIDAVIT OF APPLICANT FOR GRANT OF ADMINISTRATION WITHOUT WILL ANNEXED

I, *[name]*, of *[address]*, *[occupation]*, SWEAR (OR AFFIRM) THAT:

1   I am the applicant referred to in the submission for estate grant in relation to the estate of *[legal name of deceased]* (the "deceased") and am applying for a grant of administration without will annexed.

2.   [X]   I am an individual and ordinarily live at the following location:

City/town: *[specify]*

Province/state: *[specify]*

Country: *[specify]*

3   I am a person referred to in paragraph *[specify]* of section 130 of the *Wills, Estates and Succession Act*.

4.   [X]   I am not obliged under Rule 25-3(11) to deliver a filed copy of this submission for estate grant to the Public Guardian and Trustee.

OR

4.   [X]   I am obliged under Rule 25-3(11) to deliver a filed copy of this submission for estate grant to the Public Guardian and Trustee.

5   I am satisfied that a diligent search for a testamentary document of the deceased has been made in each place that could reasonably be considered to be a place

where a testamentary document may be found, including, without limitation, in all places where the deceased usually kept his or her documents and

    [X]   no testamentary document of the deceased has been found.

6   I believe that there is no will of the deceased.

7   [X]   I am not aware of any grant of probate or administration, or equivalent, having been issued in relation to the deceased in British Columbia or in any other jurisdiction.

8   I have read the submission for estate grant and the other documents referred to in that document and I believe that the information contained in that submission for estate grant and those documents is correct and complete.

9   I will administer according to law all of the deceased's estate, I will prepare an accounting as to how the estate was administered and I acknowledge that, in doing this, I will be subject to the legal responsibility of a personal representative.

SWORN (OR AFFIRMED))	
BEFORE ME at *[location]*,)	
British Columbia,)	
on *[month, day, year]*.)	
)	
)	
_____)	_____
A commissioner for taking affidavits)	DEPONENT'S NAME
for British Columbia)	

Nicole Garton, LLB, TEP

Form P8 (Rule 25-3(2))

This is the 1st affidavit
of *[name]* in this case and was
made on *[month, day, year]*

No.
Vancouver Registry

In the Supreme Court of British Columbia

In the Matter of the Estate of *[legal name of deceased]*, deceased

AFFIDAVIT IN SUPPORT OF APPLICATION FOR ESTATE GRANT

I, *[name]*, of *[address]*, *[occupation]*, SWEAR (OR AFFIRM) THAT:

1   I am one of the applicants referred to in the submission for estate grant in relation to the estate of *[legal name of deceased]* (the "deceased").

2   I have read the affidavit in Form *[set out whichever one of the following 5 choices is correct–P3/P4/P5/P6/P7]* sworn *[month, day, year]* by *[name of person who swore that affidavit]* and there is nothing in that affidavit that I know to be inaccurate.

3   I have read the submission for estate grant and the other documents referred to in that document and I believe that the information contained in that submission for estate grant and those documents is correct and complete.

4   I will administer according to law the deceased's estate to which the submission for estate grant relates and I acknowledge that, in doing this, I will be subject to the legal responsibility of a personal representative.

SWORN (OR AFFIRMED)	)	
BEFORE ME at *[location]*,	)	
British Columbia,	)	
on *[month, day, year]*	)	
	)	
	)	
_____	)	_____
A commissioner for taking affidavits	)	DEPONENT'S NAME
for British Columbia	)	

128

The Heritage Trust Estate Administration Boot Camp

Form P9 (Rule 25-3(2))

This is the 1st affidavit
of *[name]* in this case and was
made on *[month, day, year]*

No.
Vancouver Registry

In the Supreme Court of British Columbia

In the Matter of the Estate of *[legal name of deceased]*, deceased

AFFIDAVIT OF DELIVERY

I, *[name]*, of *[address]*, *[occupation]*, SWEAR (OR AFFIRM) THAT:

1   Attached to this affidavit and marked as Exhibit A is a copy of a notice of proposed application in Form P1 (the "notice").

2   I delivered a copy of the notice, and *[identify any other documents]* to the following persons as follows:

[ ]   by mailing it/them to the following persons by ordinary mail on *[date]*:

[name of person who received delivery by ordinary mail], a *[relationship]*,

[name of person who received delivery by ordinary mail], a *[relationship]*,

[ ]   by handing it/them to and leaving it/them with the following persons as follows on *[date]*:

[name of person who received personal delivery], a *[relationship]*,

[name of person who received personal delivery], a *[relationship]*,

[ ]   by sending it/them to the following persons by e-mail, fax or other electronic means to that person on *[date]*:

[name of person who received delivery by e-mail, fax or other electronic means], a *[relationship]*,

[name of person who received delivery by e-mail, fax or other electronic means], a *[relationship]*,

[If you checked the third of the immediately preceding 3 boxes, check both of the immediately following boxes. If you cannot check both of the immediately following boxes in relation to any person to whom the notice was sent by e-mail, fax or other electronic means, because he or she has not provided the required acknowledgement, you must re-deliver the notice and Rule 25-2(1)(b) documents by mail or personal delivery and swear to that delivery under the first or second of the boxes in this section 2.]

[ ]   Each of the persons who received delivery by e-mail, fax or other electronic means has, in writing, acknowledged receipt of the document(s) referred to in this section.

[ ]   I will retain a copy of those acknowledgements until the personal representative of the deceased is discharged and will produce those acknowledgements promptly after being requested to do so by the registrar.

SWORN (OR AFFIRMED)	)	
BEFORE ME at *[location]*,	)	
British Columbia,	)	
on *[month, day, year]*.	)	
	)	
	)	
_____	)	_____
A commissioner for taking affidavits	)	DEPONENT'S NAME
for British Columbia	)	

The Heritage Trust Estate Administration Boot Camp

Form P10 (Rule 25-3(2))

This is the 1st affidavit
of *[name]* in this case and was
made on *[month, day, year]*

No.
Vancouver Registry

In the Supreme Court of British Columbia

In the Matter of the Estate of *[legal name of deceased]*, deceased

AFFIDAVIT OF ASSETS AND LIABILITIES FOR DOMICILED ESTATE GRANT

I, *[name]*, of *[address]*, *[occupation]*, SWEAR (OR AFFIRM) THAT:

1   I am an applicant for a grant of administration without will annexed in relation to the estate of *[legal name of deceased]* (the "deceased").

2   I have made a diligent search and inquiry to find the property and liabilities of the deceased.

3   Attached to this affidavit as Exhibit A is a Statement of Assets, Liabilities and Distribution that discloses

(a)   all of the property of the deceased, irrespective of its location, nature or value, that passes to the applicant in the applicant's capacity as the deceased's personal representative,

(b)   the value of that property, and

(c)   the liabilities that charge or encumber that property.

4   If I determine that there is any property or liability that has not been disclosed in Exhibit A, I will promptly after learning of the same file an affidavit of assets and liabilities in Form P14 to disclose that information.

5.   In addition to the probate fees payable in relation to any property disclosed in Exhibit A, I promise to pay the Minister of Finance the probate fees payable with respect to the value of any property that passes to me as the deceased's personal

representative, and that is not disclosed in Exhibit A, on a determination being made as to the value of that asset.

SWORN (OR AFFIRMED)	)	
BEFORE ME at *[location]*,	)	
British Columbia,	)	
on *[month, day, year]*.	)	
	)	
	)	
_____	)	_____
A commissioner for taking affidavits	)	DEPONENT'S NAME
for British Columbia	)	

This is Exhibit A referred to in the
affidavit of *[name]* sworn
(or affirmed) before me on *[month, day, year]*.

_____

A commissioner for taking affidavits
for British Columbia

In the matter of the Estate of *[legal name of deceased]*, Deceased

STATEMENT OF ASSETS, LIABILITIES & DISTRIBUTION

Part 1 **Real Property** (including mortgages and vendors' and purchasers' interests in agreements for sale)	Within or Without British Columbia	Value at Death
Civic Address of property: Registered in the name of: Parcel Identifier: Legal Description: Appraised by: Appraised value:	Within	$
TOTAL:		**$**
Part II **Personal Property** (all assets except real property)	Within or Without British Columbia	Value at Death
A. Tangible Personal Property		
(1) Personal property, clothing and household effects No commercial value		$ 0.00
B. Intangible Personal Property		

1)			
2)			
		TOTAL:	$
		GROSS VALUE OF ESTATE:	$

Part III Liabilities	Paid or Unpaid	Amount
Unsecured Liabilities		
Secured Liabilities		
TOTAL:		$

Chapter 10

Obtaining the Estate Grant

Swearing Affidavits

When all of the documents have been prepared and reviewed, the affidavits must be sworn in front of a lawyer, notary, or commissioner for taking oaths and affidavits for British Columbia. The deponent, or person swearing the affidavit, must ensure that they have knowledge of every item listed in the affidavit and that the contents are true and accurate to the best of their knowledge and belief. If there is anything in the affidavit that the deponent is unaware of, or has not done themselves, they cannot swear the affidavit. If they do, it is technically perjury.

Checklist

Before submitting the application, ensure the following:

- The 21-day notice period has expired;

- Notice has been given to the Public Guardian and Trustee (if required), they have had the opportunity to respond to the application materials, and you have their comments to file with the estate grant application;

- All signatures and dates on documents have been completed;

- The names in the P2 Submission for Estate Grant match the names and aliases in the Wills Notice Search, and the name on the title search has been included in both;

- The original will, and codicil or any other documents referred to in the will are being filed with the application.

When you submit the estate grant application, the registry will charge you a statutory filing fee of $200.

Probate Fees

Once you have submitted the estate grant application package to the court registry, you will need to wait for the registry staff to review it. This could take considerable time depending on how busy the registry happens to be at that time. It could be anywhere from one to six months, but it is impossible to know at any given time. You can always check the status of your submission by calling the registry to see the submission date for applications they are currently working on.

The registry staff will review your package for any errors or deficiencies with the application. If they do find any deficiencies, they will list them out and send you the list so that you can correct any errors. You may need to file a supplemental affidavit or revise a document, depending on the error or deficiency. There is usually a way to correct your application without having to appear in court, unless the registry tells you otherwise.

Along with their review of your application documents, the registry will assess the amount of probate fees that are payable in relation to your estate grant. Note that a grant will not be issued without the payment of probate fees.

The *Probate Fee Act* (SBC1999, c4) governs the amount of probate fees payable. Probate fees are payable for all of the assets of the deceased that were situated within British Columbia and, with respect to all intangible assets, that were not necessarily within British Columbia but pass to the executor.

If the estate has a gross value that is under $25,000, then no probate fees are payable. Otherwise, any estate in excess of $25,000 will be charged the following:

- $6 for each $1,000 or part of $1,000 of the value of the estate in excess of $25,000, up to $50,000, and

- $14 for each $1,000 or part of $1,000 of the value of the estate in excess of $50,000.

For example, if the gross value of an estate is $125,000, the probate fee will be $1,200.

You will need to obtain a bank draft, money order, or certified cheque in the amount of your assessed probate fees, payable to the Minister of Finance. If the deceased has a bank account with enough funds to pay the probate fees, the personal representative may approach the bank with the amount of probate fees payable and ask them to issue a bank draft for the amount of fees. If the bank refuses to issue the probate fees, the personal representative may need to advance the funds and be repaid once probate has been received. Once the probate fees have been submitted and all deficiencies have been taken care of, the court registry will issue you the estate grant, plus any certified copies that you have paid for, usually within a week of paying the probate fees.

Note again that if any Notice of Dispute has been filed concerning the estate, no estate grant will be issued until that Notice of Dispute has been addressed and withdrawn. Dealing with a Notice of Dispute is beyond the scope of these materials.

Chapter 11

Post-Grant Procedures: Transfer of Assets and Distribution of the Estate

Introduction

Once you have received the estate grant, you should ensure that you store it and any certified copies of the grant in a safe place indefinitely, as it may be needed in future years to deal with matter arising from your administration of the estate.

With receipt of the grant you can now liquidate the estate assets, settle the deceased's debts, finalize income tax reporting, and prepare the documentation to distribute the estate.

If you discover any assets or liabilities that were not disclosed on the Statement of Assets, Liabilities and Distribution filed with the court (or if any information was inaccurate or incomplete), you are required to disclose that information to the court and, if applicable, pay any additional probate fees that are owing. As noted previously, you can swear a supplemental affidavit in Form P14 for this purpose.

Included at the end of this chapter is a sample Post-Grant Checklist which may be useful.

Distribution Limitation Period

WESA has a new requirement that prohibits a personal representative from distributing an estate prior to 210 days from the issuance of the estate grant, under section 155. This provides the opportunity for someone to make a variation application or bring another proceeding against the estate before a distribution has happened. This section of WESA extends to all estates, even where there are no claimants that have a right to variation.

A personal representative can, however, make a distribution or interim distribution prior to this time in certain circumstances if they can obtain the consents of all of the beneficiaries and intestate successors or if they obtain a court order. It is important to note that all beneficiaries or intestate successors who are to sign a consent should be advised that they may wish to obtain independent legal advice before doing so.

If the personal representative does not wait the allotted 210 days and distributes part or all of the estate, they may be personally liable for the loss caused by any action that is brought to vary the will provisions or by someone who has an interest in the estate. WESA has provisions that allow a child (even an adult child) or a spouse of the deceased to make an application for variation of a will where the will-maker has not made adequate provision for that child or spouse. If the application is successful, the court may make an order that allocates a different amount to that child or spouse or alter the shares between them. It is important to receive a Release and Consent from all spouses and children entitled to apply that confirms that they will not start an action. If you do discover an action has been commenced and is successful, you are personally responsible for ensuring the distributions that the court has ordered are followed. If you have already distributed funds without obtaining releases, it may be extremely difficult to get that money back from the beneficiaries, who may have already spent the money.

A sample Consent is included at the end of this chapter.

If there are children of the deceased who are minors, they are unable to sign a consent or a release. In this case, you need to ensure you wait the 210-day period without distribution.

Of course, if there is no will and you are the personal representative under an intestacy, the laws of intestacy apply. There can be no will variation action and the devolution of the estate cannot be altered.

Liquidating Assets

You are now able to liquidate the assets of the deceased, including bank accounts and investment accounts, and accumulate them into an estate account. You may need to provide certified or notarial copies of the estate grant, along with copies of the death certificate, to the financial institutions. Many financial institutions have additional requirements for transmission of assets, for example, a letter of direction and/or a Declaration of Transmission, that need to be sworn before a lawyer, notary or commissioner for taking oaths and affidavits for British Columbia.

It is prudent at this juncture to open an estate account if you have not already done so, to have all of the deceased's funds transferred into one account.

ICBC has their own checklist that charts how a motor vehicle owned by the deceased will devolve and outlines what is necessary for the transfer of that vehicle. You may need to provide them with additional documents, or to visit an Autoplan dealer in order to obtain the necessary forms.

In order to distribute land, you will need to consult with the Land Title and Survey Authority of British Columbia. You may need to transfer the land from the deceased's name into your name as personal representative or executor. In order to do this, you will need to fill out a Form 17 and attach a court-certified copy of the estate grant as well as a court-certified copy of the Statement of Assets, Liabilities and Distribution. You will also need to fill out a Property Transfer Tax Return Form, and you are able to claim an exemption for transmission to the personal representative.

You may, on the other hand, need to transfer the property to a beneficiary of the estate. In this scenario, you will still need to transfer the title into the name of the personal representative first, and then do a second title transfer to the name of the beneficiary. This second transfer will necessitate using a Form A Transfer and a Property Transfer Tax Return Form. Keep in mind that the Land Title Office requires that the deceased's name as it appears in the estate grant corresponds exactly with the title search of the property.

Once you have transmitted the financial assets to yourself as the personal representative, you can reimburse yourself for any out-of-pocket expenses incurred in your capacity as personal representative and settle the other debts and liabilities of the estate.

Creditors

Before any distribution can be made to any beneficiaries, the personal representative must pay all debts of the estate or at least hold back enough funds to ensure that all of the liabilities can be paid. If, as personal representative, you fail to pay the debts of the estate with due diligence, you could become personally liable to the creditors of the estate or the beneficiaries who lost funds due to your negligence.

There may also be contingent or continuing liabilities that are outstanding and are the responsibility of the estate. The personal representative is responsible for ensuring that these are covered by the holdback, if necessary, before distributing any funds to beneficiaries. A contingent liability might be something like an outstanding personal guarantee or a pending lawsuit. A continuing liability might be a fixed sum of ongoing child support or spousal support under a family law agreement.

Furthermore, where there is real property that has ongoing expenses payable, such as utilities or insurance payments, these payments need to be paid out of the estate funds until the real property is sold or otherwise dealt with.

The personal representative has the ability to sell any personal property of the deceased to satisfy the debts of the estate.

Section 154 of WESA states that the personal representative may publish a Notice to Creditors and Others in the *British Columbia Gazette* to afford creditors the opportunity to submit any claims against the deceased. Personal representatives advertise in the *British Columbia Gazette* to avoid becoming personally liable for any of a deceased's debts that come to their attention after the estate has been distributed to the beneficiaries. Advertising in the prescribed form does not mean that the beneficiaries can avoid valid claims by creditors, but it does help the representatives to ensure that they are not distributing estates until they have settled all the claims against the estate.

If the personal representative is completely comfortable and confident that the deceased paid all of their debts regularly, there may be nothing to warrant the publishing of a Notice to Creditors. Keep in mind that the advertising protects the personal representative from personal liability, so if there is any doubt, best practice is to publish the notice. There is a fee for advertising in the *British Columbia Gazette,* and the notice period lasts for no less than 30 days after the date that the notice was published. Therefore, if, after 30 days has elapsed from the date of publication, no creditors contact you, the creditor cannot make a claim for payment and the personal representative is essentially released from obligation to pay that creditor. The *British Columbia Gazette* runs every Thursday and the cost is $63.38 (at date of printing) for the publication of a notice. Further information can be found at online through Crown Publications.

Income Tax Returns

You should provide copies of the estate grant, the Statement of Assets, Liabilities and Distribution, and the death certificate to the accountant for the estate.

In addition to the requirement to file an income tax return on behalf of the deceased to the date of death, a T3 Trust Return must also be filed for each year or portion thereof that the estate continues in existence after the date of death. The T3 Return reports all the income earned by the estate assets, which is generally interest income from interest-bearing accounts. Consequently, at a minimum, at least one T3 Return will be required and, if it takes more than a year from the date of death to wind up the estate and make a final distribution, further T3 returns will be required for each additional year.

It is therefore important to ensure that estate funds are available to meet the tax obligations of the estate. At the point of an interim distribution, even if there appears to be no outstanding issues in the estate other than the final T3 Return, it will be necessary to hold back a portion of the assets to meet the estate's final tax liabilities, accounting fees, and legal fees. Once the time approaches to substantially distribute all of the estate, you should consult with the accountant to determine the potential tax liability and to ensure that a sufficient amount is held back.

If the personal representative fails to file such returns, pay any tax found owing, and obtain clearance certificate(s) from the Canada Revenue Agency, the personal representative may be personally responsible for payment of any tax owing by the deceased.

If you do intend to claim fees for acting as the personal representative, it is recommended that you discuss those fees with the accountant to ensure that the fees are properly reported, by both yourself and the estate, for tax purposes. Depending on your personal tax situation, the estate may be required to withhold source deductions on your fees, including income tax and Canada Pension Plan contributions, and to issue a T4 slip to you.

If there are specific trusts set-up within the will, such as a spousal trust, there may be additional tax returns that need to be prepared. You should consult with an accountant or tax professional, as intricate tax issues are beyond the scope of these materials. Other issues that might be relevant to discuss with such a professional include: graduated rate estate elections, qualified disability trusts, rights or things returns, non-resident beneficiaries, taxes owing in different jurisdictions, capital gains, donations, principal residence issues, and other testamentary trusts.

Ensure that you discuss with your accountant the need to obtain a Clearance Certificate from the Canada Revenue Agency. This is a document with respect to the deceased's tax obligations. Note that a separate certificate is required for any trust, if they exist. A Clearance Certificate should be received before the final distribution of any property under the control of the personal representative. This document states and certifies that all tax, Canada Pension Plan contributions, unemployment insurance premiums, interest, and penalties payable by the deceased have been either paid or secured to the satisfaction of the Minister of National Revenue. After the accountant or personal representative has filed all the returns necessary and paid any outstanding taxes, interest, and penalties, a Clearance Certificate can be issued for the personal representative to make a final distribution of the estate. Again, if the personal representative has distributed property before this Clearance Certificate has been issued and they have not held back enough funds to cover the costs of any outstanding amount owing, the personal representative will be personally liable for the shortfall.

Approval and Releases

You may have already had beneficiaries sign releases. A release is a contract promising that, in consideration of receiving a gift from the estate, the person signing will not make any claims against you. By signing releases, beneficiaries acknowledge receipt of their shares of the estate, approve your accounts, and release any claim that they may have against you or the estate.

If you have not yet received the releases, do so before distributing the estate.

Please note that if any beneficiary is a minor (see WESA, section 153), then additional steps (outlined in WESA, section 157(3)) must be taken before you can distribute the estate. This may include notifying the Public Guardian and Trustee or the guardian of a trust set up for the minor.

Passing of Accounts

As mentioned in Chapter 5, the personal representative has a specific responsibility to maintain and keep accounts throughout the entire estate administration process. The law requires that a personal representative be able, at any point in time, to account to the beneficiaries. They need to know what funds are available and outstanding, and they need to preserve and keep assets in trust. At the end of the estate administration process and before a final distribution is made to the beneficiaries, the personal representative must provide their accounts and show the tracing of the funds from the commencement of the estate to the final distribution. The beneficiaries must approve the accounts in writing. The accounts need to be passed within two years from the issuance of the estate grant, or at any time that the court requires it.

With reference to the law, please review section 99(1) of the *Trustee Act* (RSBC 1996, c 464):

99   (1)   Unless his or her accounts are approved and consented to in writing by all beneficiaries, or the court otherwise orders, an executor, administrator, trustee under a will and judicial trustee must, within 2 years from the date of his or her appointment, and every other trustee may at any time obtain from the court an order for passing his or her first accounts, and he or she must pass his or her subsequent accounts at the time the court directs.

The general process at this point is to provide the accounts to each beneficiary for them to approve. If they approve of the accounting, they will sign a form of release so that the distribution can occur. When there is a minor or mentally incompetent beneficiary, WESA allows a guardian of a minor or a nominee of a mentally incompetent person to consent to the accounts on their behalf, without the need to do a formal passing of accounts through the court. While the guardian or nominee can approve the accounts, they cannot sign a release on behalf of the beneficiary. Personal representatives should not distribute any portion of the estate until all beneficiaries have approved the accounts and returned a signed release.

A sample release is included at the end of this chapter for your review.

If the personal representative cannot obtain consent or approval from all of the beneficiaries (or the guardian or nominee), they must then apply for a formal passing of accounts through the court system by applying to the Registrar with a supporting affidavit in Form P38 and a statement of account affidavit in Form P40. The Registrar may decide to certify the result, and the certificate that they issue is binding on all parties. The personal representative then needs to file the documents with the court registry and arrange a date for the appointment, where they will need to appear to pass the accounts in front of the court. Before the appointment with the court, the personal representative needs to serve all the beneficiaries with the accounts, the affidavit in support, the order, and the appointment. Any beneficiary is allowed to attend at the hearing if they so choose. At the end of the hearing, the Registrar must then certify the results of the hearing and then the certificate.

The following are all included in the accounting:

- Details of the assets and liabilities as at the date of death;

- Details of each receipt and disbursement during the administration of estate;

- A list of the assets the representative now has on hand;

- A calculation of the remuneration, if sought; and

- A statement of the proposed distribution.

The estate accounts should include a reserve or a holdback, as described earlier, and the amount of income tax should be determined with the advice of the accountant.

As mentioned in the list above, the estate accounts should detail the personal representative's claim for remuneration in acting in that capacity. The basis of this remuneration may come from a clause in the will that provides a sum for the executor, there may be a compensation agreement to refer to, or the personal representative may rely on the *Trustee Act* in order to claim a percentage of the estate. Refer to section 88 of the *Trustee Act* (RSBC 1996, c 464):

88 (1) A trustee under a deed, settlement or will, an executor or administrator, a guardian appointed by any court, a testamentary guardian, or any other trustee, however the trust is created, is entitled to, and it is lawful for the Supreme Court, or a registrar of that court if so directed by the court, to allow him or her a fair and reasonable allowance, not exceeding 5% on the gross aggregate value, including capital and income, of all the assets of the estate by way of remuneration for his or her care, pains and trouble and his or her time spent in and about the trusteeship, executorship, guardianship or administration of the estate and effects vested in him or her under any will or grant of administration, and in administering, disposing of and arranging and settling the same, and generally in arranging and settling the affairs of the estate as the court, or a registrar of the court if so directed by the court thinks proper.

(3) A person entitled to an allowance under subsection (1) may apply annually to the Supreme Court for a care and management fee and the court may allow a fee not exceeding 0.4% of the average market value of the assets.

Therefore, while the maximum allowable compensation for a personal representative is 5% that is very seldom claimed. The basis for determining the appropriate percentage has been developed through case law and the factors to consider are as follows:

- The magnitude of the trust;

- The care and responsibility involved;

- The time spent to administer the estate;

- The skill and ability displayed; and

- The success achieved in the administration of the estate.

The Supreme Court uses the Form in P40 to chart all of the above information. A sample Form P40 is included at the end of this chapter for your review.

POST-GRANT CHECKLIST

		N/A	Required	Completed (date)
1.	Receive estate grant			
2.	Advertise for creditors			
3.	Prepare notarial copies of grant			
4.	Complete insurance/annuity/pension claims			
5.	Arrange for transmission/transfer/sale of specific assets to meet cash needs			
6.	Transfer assets held in joint tenancy and with designated beneficiary to surviving joint tenant or appropriate beneficiary			
7.	Arrange for payment of cash legacies/specific bequests			
8.	Arrange for payment of debts			
9.	Arrange for transmissions/transfer/sale of remaining assets			
10.	Arrange for preparation and filing of all Income Tax Returns Name of Accountants:			
11.	Apply for Clearance Certificate			
12.	Clearance Certificate received			
13.	Reserve funds for: Personal Representative fee $_____ Solicitor's billing $_____ Accountants billing $_____ Income Tax $_____			
14.	Prepare Trust Reconciliation Statement			
15.	Prepare Releases and Receipts			
16.	Send letter to residuary beneficiaries with Releases			
17.	Receive all Releases and pay residue of estate			
18.	Account for tax reserve or other holdback			

CONSENT

In the Matter of the Estate of
[name of deceased], Deceased (the "Estate") and
the Wills Estates and Succession Act, Subsections 69(1) and 155(1)

WHEREAS:

A. *[Name of deceased]*, last of *[address]*, *[occupation]*, died on *[month, day, year]* at *[city, province]*, leaving a will dated *[month, day, year]*.

B. A representation grant was issued on *[month, day, year]* in the Supreme Court of British Columbia, *[location]* Registry, confirming the appointment of *[name of executor/administrator]* as *[executor of the will/administrator of the estate]* (the "Grant").

C. Subsections 69(1) and 155(1) of the Wills, Estates and Succession Act provide that an estate of a deceased person cannot be distributed in the 210 days following the date of issue of the representation grant except with the consent of all beneficiaries and intestate successors entitled to the estate or by court order.

D. The beneficiaries and intestate successors are *[list persons, relationships to deceased (if known), and whether they are entitled to the estate of the deceased as beneficiaries or intestate successors, or both]*.

Pursuant to subsection 155(1) of the Wills, Estates and Succession Act, I, *[name of person]*, declare:

1. I am a *[beneficiary/intestate successor]* of the Estate.

2. I hereby consent to the transfer and distribution forthwith (and within 210 days following the date of issue of the Grant) of the following assets to the following *[beneficiaries/intestate successors]*:

    [list assets and beneficiaries]

3. I acknowledge that I am aware of my right to seek legal advice with respect to the content and effect of this Consent before executing the same, and that I have either obtained such legal advice or knowingly declined to do so.

DATED at *[city, province]*, *[month, day, year]*.

SIGNED by *[name of person entitled]*,
[day, month, year] in the presence of:

_____

Witness signature   *[Name of Beneficiary/Intestate Successor]*

_____

Witness name

_____

Address

_____

Occupation

FINAL RELEASE AND APPROVAL OF ACCOUNTS

FOR THE PERIOD OF *[DATE]* TO *[DATE]*

In the matter of the Estate of *[name]* (the "Deceased"), of *[city]*, British Columbia, who died on the *[day]* of *[month, year]*.

KNOW ALL PERSONS BY THESE PRESENTS that I, *[name]*, of *[city, province]*, a residual beneficiary of the Deceased's Will, DO HEREBY:

1. Acknowledge that I have received from *[personal representative name]* a statement of *[his/her]* receipts and disbursements in *[his/her]* capacity as *[executor/ administrator]* of the Deceased's estate (the "Statement of Accounts"), a copy of which is attached to this Final Release and Approval of Accounts, and I approve this Statement of Accounts and waive the formal passing of accounts by *[personal representative name]*.

2. Acknowledge that I will receive from *[personal representative name]* the sum of $*[amount]* as my pro rata share of the final distribution of the assets of the Deceased's estate, upon all residual beneficiaries approving this Statement of Accounts;

3. Remise, release, and forever discharge *[personal representative name]* and *[his/ her]* heirs, executors, administrators, and assigns of and from all manner of actions, suits, payments, accounts, reckonings, claims, and demands whatsoever against the estate and its assets, and concerning the management and disposition of the estate;

4. Do by these presents agree to indemnify, to the extent of my pro rata share of the residue of the Deceased's estate, *[personal representative name]* for any amount of income taxes, succession duties or any other sum for which *[he/she]* may be held personally liable, by virtue of *[his/her]* administration of the Deceased's estate. I agree to this right of indemnification regardless of whether *[he/she]* has obtained the requisite certificate described under the Income Tax Act.

PROVIDED HOWEVER THAT this Release shall not include any assets, which may in the future come into the hands of *[personal representative name]* and form part of the Deceased's Estate.

IN WITNESS WHEREOF I have hereunto set my hand and seal this *[day]* day of *[month, year]*.

SIGNED, SEALED and DELIVERED in
the presence of:

_____

Witness name

_____

Address

_____

Occupation

_____

[Name]

Nicole Garton, LLB, TEP

STATEMENT OF ACCOUNT FOR THE ESTATE OF
[deceased], DECEASED

For the period from *[commencement date]* to *[effective date]*.

1. In this Statement of Account, the "commencement date" means

    (a) the deceased's date of death, or

    (b) if one or more statements of account have been filed in respect of the estate under Rule 25-13(6) of the Supreme Court Civil Rules, the effective date of the most recent of those statements of account.

2. This Statement of Account consists of the following:

    (a) Statement of Assets and Liabilities of the Estate of *[deceased]* as at *[commencement date]*;

    (b) Statement of Capital Transactions of the Estate of *[deceased]*;

    (c) Statement of Income Transactions of the Estate of *[deceased]*;

    (d) Statement of Assets and Liabilities of the Estate of *[deceased]* as at *[effective date]*;

    (e) *[include only if remuneration is sought at this time]* Statement of Proposed Remuneration in relation to the Estate of *[deceased]*;

    (f) Statement of Distribution of the Estate of *[deceased]*

    (g) Statement of Proposed Distribution of Residue of the Estate of *[deceased]*.

STATEMENT OF ASSETS AND LIABILITIES OF
THE ESTATE OF *[deceased]*

AS AT *[commencement date]*

Item	Assets	Asset Values
A1		
A2		
		Total asset values $ *[specify]*

Item	Liabilities	Liabilities
B1		
B2		
		Total amount of liabilities $ *[specify]*

STATEMENT OF CAPITAL TRANSACTIONS
OF THE ESTATE OF *[deceased]*
FOR THE PERIOD FROM *[commencement date]*
TO *[effective date]*

Item	Date	Transaction	Debit	Credit
C1				
C2				
			Total of debits $ *[specify]*	Total of credits $ *[specify]*

STATEMENT OF INCOME TRANSACTIONS
OF THE ESTATE OF *[deceased]*

FOR THE PERIOD FROM *[commencement date]*
TO *[effective date]*

Item	Date	Transaction	Debit	Credit
D1				
D2				
			Total of debits $ *[specify]*	Total of credits $ *[specify]*

STATEMENT OF ASSETS AND LIABILITIES
OF THE ESTATE OF *[deceased]*
AS AT *[effective date]*

Item	Assets	Asset Values
E1		
E2		
		Total asset values $ *[specify]*

Item	Liabilities	Liability Values
F1		
F2		
		Total amount of liabilities $ *[specify]*

STATEMENT OF PROPOSED REMUNERATION
IN RELATION TO THE ESTATE OF *[deceased]*

Capital Fee		
(A)	Proceeds of disposition of capital assets realized since the commencement date	$ *[specify]*
(B)	Market value of capital assets, realized or transferred since the commencement date, in respect of which no proceeds of disposition have been obtained	$ *[specify]*
(C)	Current value of unrealized capital assets included, on the commencement date, in the estate	$ *[specify]*
(D)	Gross aggregate value of capital assets of estate – [(A) + (B) + (C)]	$ *[specify]*
(E)	Capital Fee – (D) x % *[insert claimed percentage, up to a maximum of 5%]*	$ *[specify]*
Income Fee		
(F)	Gross income earned by the estate for period from *[commencement date—month, day, year]* to *[effective date of this statement of account—month, day, year]* except interest income already capitalized and included in (D)	$ *[specify]*
(G)	Income Fee – (F) x % *[insert claimed percentage, up to a maximum of 5%]*	$ *[specify]*

Care and Management Fee		
[Prepare one set of the following calculations for each reporting period following the commencement date, where a reporting period is each calendar year, or portion, from date of death to the date of final distribution.]		
(H)	Market value of estate assets as at the beginning of the reporting period	$ *[specify]*
(I)	Market value of estate assets at the end of the reporting period	$ *[specify]*
(J)	Average market value of estate assets for the reporting period [(H) + (I)] / 2	$ *[specify]*
(K)	Care and Management Fee for reporting period [(J) x 0.4%]	$ *[specify]*

Total of Fees Claimed		
(L)	Total remuneration sought – [(E) + (G) + (the total of every (K) determined for a reporting period following the commencement date)]	$ *[specify]*

STATEMENT OF DISTRIBUTION OF THE ESTATE OF *[deceased]*

SPECIFIC BEQUESTS AND LEGACIES

Item	Distribution (Yes/No)	Date of distribution	Beneficiary

RESIDUE OF ESTATE

(R1)	Market value of estate assets at effective date of this statement of account	$ *[specify]*
(R2)	Applicant's estimated reserve for final income tax, accounting and legal costs and remuneration	$ *[specify]*
(R3)	Distributable estate (R1)–(R2)	$ *[specify]*

STATEMENT OF PROPOSED DISTRIBUTION
OF RESIDUE OF THE ESTATE OF *[specify]*

Beneficiary	Assets	Cash
[Name]		$ *[specify]*
[Name]		$ *[specify]*
[Name]		$ *[specify]*
[Name]		$ *[specify]*

Chapter 12

Your Role as the Trustee

The trustee acts as the legal owner of trust assets and is responsible for handling the assets held in trust, completing tax filings for the trust, and distributing the assets according to the terms of the trust to the beneficiaries.

The obligations of a trustee apply to all trusts. You may come across an "ongoing trust" in your time as a trustee. Note that an "ongoing trust" is not a separate kind of trust; this is a term used to describe a trust that operates for an extended period of time. An ongoing trust will usually provide detailed instructions for how trust assets should be used.

As a trustee you will be held to a high standard and may be personally liable for any mistakes made. You may also face pressure and demands from the beneficiaries.

A person who has been named or appointed as a trustee may disclaim the role and is then not required to act. However, a person who has already accepted the role of trustee cannot then disclaim the role and must instead seek a discharge. That person will still be required to account for all dealings with the trust property from the point of acceptance to resignation.

Obligations of the trustee include:

- Acting within the scope of the trust. The only exception to this is if the trust provisions are illegal, impossible to meet, or uncertain;

- Ensuring that the assets are safe and under your control, that you understand the terms of the trust and who the beneficiaries are, and that all past account records are in order;

- Investing the trust assets (if applicable) in such a way as to make sure the assets are preserved and productive for current and future beneficiaries;

- Administering the trust according to its terms, including distributing trust assets to the beneficiaries according to the trust agreement;

- Preparing any records, statements, and tax returns as needed – pursuant to section 230 of the *Income Tax Act* (RSC 1985, c. 1), a trust is like any other tax paying entity and is required to keep records and books of accounts (it is best practice to keep documents for a minimum of 6 years);

- Communicating regularly with beneficiaries, including issuing statements of accounts and tax reports; and,

- Treating beneficiaries impartially.

If there is uncertainty as to the interpretation of the trust, the trustee may apply to the court for direction pursuant to section 86 of the *Trustee Act* (RSBC 1996 c 464). This can delay the timeline and add unwanted costs; however, going to the court for direction can relieve a trustee from personal liability (section 87 of the *Trustee* Act).

Note that if the trustee relied on legal advice without obtaining direction from the court, then said trustee can be held to be personally liable if the legal opinion is found to be incorrect. When deciding whether to seek direction from the court, you should consider the certainty of the legal opinion sought, the consequences of relying on the opinion, and consensus surrounding the opinion.

As a fiduciary, you must be loyal to the beneficiaries and avoid all conflicts of interest. A conflict of interest can arise if you, as the trustee, sell or loan trust assets to yourself or to the trust. A conflict of interest can also arise if you, the trustee, obtain a profit or benefit from the trust property.

It is important to remember that you cannot delegate your trustee duties. Delegation is allowed only when specifically permitted by law or as outlined by the terms of the trust.

Chapter 13

Estates of Indigenous People

There are specific provisions in the *Indian Act* (RSC 1985 c 1-5) that set out a complete code pertaining to the testamentary matters of Indigenous people who are registered (or entitled to be registered) as "Indians" under the *Indian Act*.

The estate of an Indigenous or First Nations person might involve special considerations:

- Settling the estate could be governed by the federal *Indian Act*, not WESA;

- Devises of real property on reserve could fail, or involve other Band members and require approval of the Minister of Indigenous and Northern Affairs;

- Gifts of personal property could include cultural artefacts (such as art, carvings, or masks), and disposition of cultural artefacts raises special concerns and potential liability for the executor; and

- Probate could require approval of the Minister of Indigenous and Northern Affairs.

If the testator lived on reserve, it is best to contact Indigenous and Northern Affairs Canada at 1-800-567-9604 or aadnc.infopubs.aandc@canada.ca

WESA applies to the estates of Nisga'a citizens (WESA, sections 13-18.3) and could also apply to the estates of other Indigenous persons whose First Nation has executed a treaty and land claims final agreement with the federal and provincial governments and become a "treaty First Nation" in BC.

WESA (section 14) allows a treaty First Nation to be involved in an estate proceeding if the estate includes cultural property in order to ensure that the property is dealt with in ways that respect the treaty First Nation's cultural laws or traditions. WESA (section 14) also allows a treaty First Nation to become involved if there is a dispute about validity or variation of the will.

If there is a property interest in reserve land, section 50 of *the Indian Act* applies. A person who is not entitled to reside on the reserve cannot receive reserve property. If the testator leaves property on reserve to an individual who is not entitled to reserve property, then the property can be sold. The proceeds of the sale will be given to the beneficiary.

If the testator dies intestate, the order outlined in section 48 of the *Indian Act* will apply. The first $75,000 of the estate will go to the surviving spouse. If there is excess, the residue will be split between the spouse and children *per stirpes*. If there is no surviving spouse, then the estate will pass to the children *per stirpes*.

The Government of Canada has published a detailed guide on administering an *Indian Act* estate. It can be found at: https://www.aadnc-aandc.gc.ca/DAM/DAM-INTER-HQ-BR/ STAGING/texte-text/br_es_adminAestate_1336489606902_eng.pdf

Chapter 14

Closing Matters

As a final check, when the following tasks have been completed, the executor's or administrator's work is finished:

- A Notice to Creditors was published (if necessary), and the time for creditors to come forward has elapsed,

- All debts and claims have been paid,

- A clearance certificate was obtained from the Canada Revenue Agency,

- The beneficiaries have provided releases,

- If security or a bond was required, it has been cancelled,

- All estate assets have been distributed to the beneficiaries,

- An accounting has been provided to beneficiaries and some creditors.

This brings us to the end of the guide. By this point you will have executed or administered estate. If there are continuing legal obligations, like being a trustee, ensure that you are aware of you rights and responsibilities. If any questions arise, it is always advisable to seek legal direction.

Further Resources

Although many resources have been listed throughout this guide, we have included a list of additional online sources below for your convenience.

- BC Courts website – provides fact sheets on court proceedings

- British Columbia Law Institute, *Report on Common-Law Tests of Capacity* (2013)

- "Following a Death" – provides information about Canada Pension Plan, death benefits under the Plan, and steps following a death

- Canada Revenue Agency, *What to Do When Someone Has Died*

- Canada Revenue Agency, IC82-6R10, *Information Circular on Asking for a Clearance Certificate*

- Canada Revenue Agency, *Guide T4011: Preparing Returns for Deceased Persons*

- Canadian Bar Association. "The Disappointed Beneficiary"

- Continuing Legal Education Society of BC. "*Wills Variation Act* Update"

- Heritage Law, "Remuneration of the Personal Representative"

- Heritage Law's website – contains current information on estate administration

- Justice Education Society booklet, *Starting a Proceeding by Petition*

- Law Society of BC, "Probate and Administration Procedure"

- People's Law School booklet, *Being an Executor*

Terms and Definitions

Administrator: Where there is no will, the court appoints someone, usually a family member or friend of the deceased, as an administrator. The administrator gathers and distributes the estate assets, performing what is called "administration of the estate".

Affidavit: A written statement of facts that is signed by the person who knows the facts to be true. It is witnessed by a lawyer, notary, or other commissioner for taking affidavits.

Attestation clause: A clause in a will that describes the signing of the will, specifying that the witnesses were both present when the will-maker signed the will, and that they signed it in the presence of the will-maker (WESA, section 37).

Beneficiary: A person who receives a gift or benefit from the estate. A person may be named in the will as a beneficiary or may have a beneficial interest in estate assets.

Bequest: A gift of personal property set out in the will. It is typically distinguished from a devise, which is a gift of real property. It may be a general entitlement, or it may be a specific bequest.

Bond: A guarantee or indemnity obtained from an insurer. An executor or administrator may be required by a court to obtain a bond before being allowed to gather and distribute estate assets.

Capital gain: Increase in the value of an asset between the date of purchase and the date when the asset is sold. The date of sale may be deemed to be the date of the will-maker's death.

Citation: A form (P32) requiring the executor to apply to the court for probate. If that person fails to apply for probate, he or she is deemed to have renounced executorship. An answer to a Citation is filed in Form P33.

Certificate: If the registrar conducts an investigation of the accounts as part of the procedure described in Rule 25-13 for the passing of accounts, the registrar completes the certificate in Form P39.

Clearance certificate: A tax clearance certificate from the Canada Revenue Agency confirms that all income taxes or fees of the estate are paid.

Codicil: An addition to the will (usually a separate document attached to the will), which must be witnessed in the same manner as the original will.

Committee: A person appointed under the *Patient's Property Act* (RSBC 1996, c 349) or pursuant to Part 2.1 of the *Adult Guardianship Act* (RSBC 1996, c 6) to look after the finances or well-being of a person who is incapable of doing so.

Court: Claims under WESA must be brought to the Supreme Court of British Columbia, but other matters, such as family disputes that do not include divorce, may go before the Provincial Court of British Columbia.

Death certificate: A certificate issued by the BC Vital Statistics Agency.

Designated beneficiary: A beneficiary named in a benefit plan, such as a workplace pension plan, a TFSA (tax-free savings account), or an RRSP.

Devise: A gift of real property described in a will.

Digital assets: Assets in online accounts, which may include Bitcoin, photo albums on Facebook, documents in DropBox, loyalty points (such as Air Miles), or online credits (such as credit balances in an Amazon account).

Estate: In general, this refers to the assets and financial affairs of the deceased.

Executor: The person who gathers the assets of the estate, pays off the estate debts, and distributes the remaining assets, (also called the "personal representative").

Executor's year: The executor (also called the "personal representative") is generally given a year from the date of the deceased's death to distribute the deceased's estate to the beneficiaries. For complicated estates it can take longer.

Graduated rate estate: A testamentary trust available for up to 36 months following the testator's death that would be taxed at graduated rates instead of at the highest marginal rate. It may have a year-end for tax purposes that is not the end of the calendar year.

Grant of probate: A court or registrar will make a grant (sometimes also called an estate grant or a representation grant) naming a person who is responsible for winding up the estate, paying the deceased's debts, and distributing the deceased's assets. If there is a will, the grant is a grant of probate and the person named to represent the deceased is the executor.

Inter vivos trust: A trust created by the will-maker during his or her lifetime. It is different from a testamentary trust that is created in the will.

Intestate: Without a will. WESA (sections 19-25) sets out the rules for how to divide an estate where there is no will. Partial intestacy (WESA, section 25) may occur if there is a will but it only deals with part of the estate. The portion not covered by the will is distributed according to the rules for intestacy.

Lapse: If the beneficiary dies before the will-maker, a gift in a will to that beneficiary is said to lapse.

Legacy: A benefit conferred or received after death, whether described in a will or not.

Letters of administration: Where there is no will, a person who proposes to administer the estate (gather and distribute the estate assets) applies to the court for a grant of letters of administration.

Letters of administration (with will annexed): Where there is a will but the named executor is unable to act or is a minor, a person who proposes to administer the estate applies to the court for a grant of letters of administration (with will annexed).

Letters probate: When a court confirms that the will is valid, the grant of probate is sometimes called "letters probate".

Military will: A will made by a person of any age (WESA, section 38) while on active service in the armed forces. It may be signed without being witnessed. Proof may be required that the will-maker was entitled to execute the will in the manner (Rule 25-3(17)).

Minor: A person under the age of majority, which is currently 19 in British Columbia (*Age of Majority Act*, [RSBC 1996, c. 7]). Note that a will can be valid in BC if the will-maker is 16-year or older and mentally capable of making a will, or a minor who executes a military will.

Next-of-kin: The closest living relative. This designation becomes relevant in intestate succession.

Nominee: A person who acts on behalf of the will-maker under a power of attorney or a representation agreement.

Notice to Creditors: A notice published in the *BC Gazette* advising creditors to make known if they have claims against the estate.

Notice of Dispute: A form (Form P29) to notify the court that a person (the "disputant") opposes a grant (e.g., the disputant has reason to believe that the will is invalid or incomplete, or that the person applying is not the proper person to apply).

Official administrator: If there is no will naming an executor and no relative or friend of the deceased who is able to apply to administer the estate, the Public Guardian and Trustee will act as the official administrator of the estate.

Per capita at each generation and per stirpes: Literally, "per capita" means "by the head" and "per stirpes" means "by the foot." These are different ways of dividing assets. When a parent leaves assets to children "per stirpes," it means that each living child gets an equal share, but if one of those children is already deceased, then that child's share is divided between his or her own children. When a parent leaves assets "per capita at each generation," it means that each living child gets what would be an equal share, but if one or more children are already deceased when the will-maker dies, the entire amount that would have gone to those deceased children is divided equally (per capita) amongst all those deceased children's surviving children.

For example, see the following chart showing distribution of a parent's assets where 2 of 3 children have died before the parent:

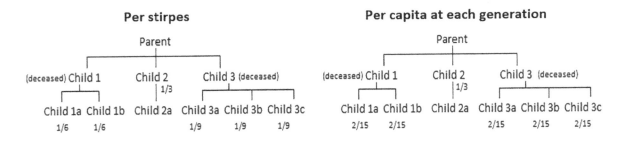

Personal representative: The executor or administrator of an estate.

Power of attorney: A document signed by an adult giving an agent or "attorney" the power to handle that adult's legal and financial affairs.

Probate: The court process to confirm that a will is valid. The court issues an order that is sometimes called a "grant of probate" or "letters probate."

Proof in common form: Approval of a will by a registrar of the court where there are no irregularities with the will or apparent disputes over it.

Proof in solemn form: A proceeding used when there is a dispute (or potential dispute) as to a will's validity.

Public Guardian and Trustee: The Public Guardian and Trustee protects the interests of vulnerable British Columbians. The Public Guardian and Trustee provides guardianship and trust services, and their powers are set out in several statutes.

Rectification: Correcting an error. A court may be called upon to "rectify" what appears to be an error in a will.

Renunciation: Literally "refusal", used in the sense of a person who has the right to be executor giving up or "renouncing" that right.

Representation grant: An estate grant, or a grant of probate, or a grant of letters of administration, or an order resealing a grant.

Representative: Person designated to make decisions on behalf of a person who has executed a representation agreement under the *Representation Agreement Act*.

Residuary beneficiary: A beneficiary who receives a gift from the estate residue.

Residue: The remaining assets of the estate after all the debts have been paid and the specific gifts have been distributed.

Revocation: Cancellation. A will that the will-maker decides no longer represents his or her wishes is revoked when the will-maker makes a new will (WESA, section 55). The will-maker may file a wills notice revoking a prior will. An estate grant can be revoked (WESA, section 141) in some circumstances.

Safety deposit box: A locked box rented to store valuables in a vault at a financial institution (bank, credit union, trust company). Many people choose to store their wills in a safety deposit box.

Specific bequest: A gift of a particular amount of money or personal property described in a will.

Specific devise: A gift of a particular piece of real property described in a will.

Spousal home: A residence where the deceased person and his or her spouse ordinarily lived, as defined in WESA (section 1). If the spousal home is not a gift in the will and the surviving spouse intends to purchase the home or continue living there (WESA, sections 26-35), that spouse must notify the executor in Form P42 within 180 days of the grant of probate being issued (WESA, section 27). (If there is a dispute over the spouse's entitlement, you should seek legal advice.)

Spouse: Spouses are people who were married to each other at the date of death or had been living together in a marriage-like relationship for a period of two or more years immediately prior to the date of death.

Succession: The order of entitlement to inherit. It usually arises where there is no will or where a gift under a will cannot be made to the beneficiary set out in the will and goes to the person whose is next in line to inherit.

Survivor: Literally, one who survives another. It often refers a spouse after the passing of the other spouse, resulting in terms like "rules of survivorship" or "survivor pensions."

Testamentary trust: A trust created in a will, where the will specifies who will be the trustee, who will be the beneficiary, and what assets are set aside for the trust.

Will-maker: The person who makes a will. Some older language identifies a male will-maker as a "testator" and a female will-maker as a "testatrix." Under WESA, any person who makes a will is called a "will-maker".

Will: A formal document describing how the writer's assets are to be divided after the writer's death. A will may have one or more codicils. To be valid, a will must follow some formal rules.

Wills notice: A notice filed at the Vital Statistics Agency in Victoria informing of the existence of a will and where it is located.

Like this?	Short Reads		Medium Reads		Long Reads	
The Handmaid's Tale	❏	"The Story of an Hour"	❏	"Silly Novels by Lady Novelists"	❏	The Yellow Wallpaper
	❏	"On Nomination to the Supreme Court"	❏	"Women's Rights are Human Rights"	❏	Emma (Abridged)
Stranger Things	❏	"Ex Oblivione"	❏	"An Occurrence at Owl Creek Bridge"	❏	The Pit and the Pendulum
			❏	"2-B-R-0-2-B"		
The Outdoors	❏	"Yosemite Fall"	❏	"Where I Lived, And What I Lived For"	❏	To Build a Fire
Satire	❏	"Advice to Youth"	❏	"A Modest Proposal"	❏	Three Satirical Short Stories from Saki
Math and Science	❏	Flatland	❏	On Marie Curie's Discovery of Radium (paired)	❏	Earthquakes
	❏	The Dangers of Spaceflight (paired)				
House of Cards	❏	"The King of Vultures"	❏	Macbeth: A Prose Adaptation	❏	"The Fad of the Fisherman"
	❏	Selection from The Prince				
Comic Book Movies	❏	The Young Edda	❏	A History of the Amazons	❏	An Essay on the Principle of Population
Parks and Recreation	❏	"Yosemite Fall"	❏	"Government is the Problem"	❏	The Inaugural Addresses of Abraham Lincoln
			❏	"Women's Rights are Human Rights"		
Hamilton	❏	"On My Impending Duel with Aaron Burr" (paired)	❏	On the Separation of Power (paired)	❏	The Farmer and the Farmer Refuted (paired)
Science Fiction and Dystopian Literature	❏	The War of the Worlds	❏	"2-B-R-0-2-B"	❏	The Hanging Stranger
	❏	The Dangers of Spaceflight (paired)	❏	"The Pendulum"		
Game of Thrones and Lord of the Rings	❏	The Young Edda	❏	"Macbeth: A Prose Adaptation"	❏	The Death of King Arthur (Le Morte d'Arthur)
	❏	Selection from The Prince				
Literature	❏	"The Story of an Hour"	❏	Macbeth: A Prose Adaptation	❏	Emma (Abridged)
African American History	❏	"What to the Slave Is the Fourth of July?"	❏	Editorials from The Crisis (paired)	❏	"Letter from Birmingham Jail"
The American Revolution	❏	"On My Impending Interview with Burr" (paired)	❏	"On the Separation of Powers" (paired)	❏	The Farmer and the Farmer Refuted (paired)
The American Civil War	❏	"What to the Slave Is the Fourth of July?"	❏	"An Occurrence at Owl Creek Bridge"	❏	The Inaugural Addresses of Abraham Lincoln (paired)
The Cold War	❏	"Don't Wait for the Translation!"	❏	"Ich bin ein Berliner" and "Tear Down this Wall" (paired)	❏	National Security Council Report 68
Economics	❏	"The Division of Labor"	❏	"Government is the Problem"	❏	On the Principle of Population
Philosophy	❏	"The King of Vultures"	❏	"Where I Lived, And What I Lived For"	❏	On the Principle of Population